Teens for Literacy

Promoting Reading and Writing in Schools and Communities

Allen Berger
Miami University
Oxford, Ohio, USA

Elizabeth A. Shafran
Mason City Schools
Mason, Ohio, USA

INTERNATIONAL
Reading
Association

800 Barksdale Road, PO Box 8139
Newark, Delaware 19714-8139, USA
www.reading.org

The International Reading Association attempts, through its publications, to provide a forum for a wide spectrum of opinions on reading. This policy permits divergent viewpoints without implying the endorsement of the Association.

Director of Publications Joan M. Irwin
Assistant Director of Publications Jeanette K. Moss
Editor in Chief, Books Matthew W. Baker
Permissions Editor Janet S. Parrack
Associate Editor Tori Mello
Assistant Editor Sarah Rutigliano
Acquisitions and Communications Coordinator Amy T. Roff
Publications Coordinator Beth Doughty
Association Editor David K. Roberts
Production Department Manager Iona Sauscermen
Art Director Boni Nash
Electronic Publishing Supervisor Wendy A. Mazur
Electronic Publishing Specialist Anette Schütz-Ruff
Electronic Publishing Specialist Cheryl J. Strum
Electronic Publishing Assistant Jeanine K. McGann

Project Editor Matthew W. Baker

Photo Credits Image Productions, cover

Copyright 2000 by the International Reading Association, Inc.
All rights reserved. No part of this publication may be reproduced or transmitted in any form or by any means, electronic or mechanical, including photocopy, or any informational storage and retrieval system, without permission from the publisher.

Library of Congress Cataloging in Publication Data
Berger, Allen.
　　Teens for literacy: promoting reading and writing in schools and communities/Allen Berger, Elizabeth Shafran.
　　　　p.　　cm.
　　Includes bibliographical references (p.).
　　ISBN 0-87207-255-X
　　1. Literacy programs—United States.　2. Peer-group tutoring of students—United States.　I. Shafran, Elizabeth.　II. Title.
LC151.B47　　2000　　　　　　　　　　　　　　　　　　　　　　99-051611
302.2'244—dc21

This book is for Carmen and Charlene Trovato,

friends and educators

and Andy Shafran, Mike and Karen Muska

Contents

Foreword

More than a decade ago while serving as Director of University Gifts for Miami University, I met a local bank president named Robert Wills. He posed to me a most interesting question: "What is the most pressing concern facing the United States today?" I paused for a moment as dozens of ideas flashed through my mind. Caught off guard, I answered, "illiteracy." Then having to justify my answer, I proceeded with logical responses. The more I talked, the more I was convinced, in my own mind, that an alarming statistic is the percentage of the United States population who cannot read or write.

The Teens for Literacy program emerged to encourage inner-city middle school and junior high school students to become involved in promoting literacy in their own schools and communities. *Teens for Literacy: Promoting Reading and Writing in Schools and Communities* is a result of the authors' experience with this program. Throughout this book, authors Allen Berger and Elizabeth Shafran describe how the Teens for Literacy program unfolds into a sequence of proactive initiatives, with middle school and junior high school teachers actively participating. The teachers in this program guide teens who help their peers and younger children, many of whom come from single-parent homes. As the school year progresses, the tutoring relationship flourishes with patience, love, and caring persistence. The results each year of Teens for Literacy are remarkable and measurable as children learn to read with greater confidence gained through guidance and practice.

My involvement with the Teens for Literacy program began more than 10 years ago when I introduced myself to Allen Berger.

From our conversations about literacy came the belief that teens must take responsibility for the improvement of their education. Over the years Allen and I have examined and re-examined what works and does not work in inner-city schools. When Allen goes into inner-city schools to help teachers establish a new program, he does not ask to meet only with good readers; he asks for students who can work together. The teams of teens that are formed are often made up of students with diverse ethnic backgrounds, all of whom work closely with one another.

Several times Allen has asked me to talk about the Teens for Literacy program at International Reading Association conventions. What impressed me at these presentations was not only the great interest among teachers who taught in inner-city schools but also the number of teachers from suburban and rural schools who expressed interest in starting the program where they taught.

Although successful in my professional career as a fundraiser, nothing has given me greater satisfaction than finding donors who each year enjoy financially supporting the Teens for Literacy program. With financial support from university donors and with the help of dedicated faculty and graduate assistants, teams of students have emerged able to participate in daily activities such as tutoring, reading aloud, making audiotapes and videotapes to encourage reading, and following students on a university campus. All these activities are described in this practical book.

I am more strongly convinced than ever that a learned population—one knowing how to read, write, and comprehend—is a nation's greatest asset. Students must learn to know letters through sound, and they must be able to read with meaning and fluency. What better gift to a child than people of all ages who can read to disseminate information. That is why *Teens for Literacy* is a gift and investment in our future. What Allen and Elizabeth have written is an easy-to-read book that can be used to improve reading and writing in schools throughout the world.

Henry Jung
Director of University Gifts (retired)
Miami University
Oxford, Ohio, USA

Acknowledgments

We wish to thank all the principals, teachers, and students in the Teens for Literacy program. In particular, we thank Ed Jung, principal, and Patricia Priore, teacher, for letting us "hang out" in Porter Middle School, Cincinnati, Ohio. We also thank Kelley Loetscher for permitting us ongoing observation in her classroom in Schwab Middle School, Cincinnati.

For sharing additional insights we extend our appreciation to Becky Lawson, Garfield Junior High in Hamilton, Ohio, and to Phil Wyly, principal, Burton Elementary School, Cincinnati.

Special thanks goes to Henry Jung, retired Director of Gifts and Divisional Support, Miami University. Henry epitomizes and personifies the finest qualities of a businessman and educator. Because of him, our program began and was sustained through alumni gifts until his retirement.

We also wish to thank Miami University alumni for their contributions to the Teens for Literacy program.

The program also has been blessed by graduate assistants who have made important contributions: Laura Bunker (who thought of Shadowing Day), Michelle Iserson Korman, and Kathy Priore. We also would like to thank Mary Fuller, codirector, Ohio Writing Project, for taking the time to read an early draft of this book.

Research references and tips on tutoring came from Doug Green and Joan Krabbe of the Office of Learning Assistance, Miami University.

Systematic ways to observe in schools came from Donna Alvermann and Penny Oldfather of the University of Georgia.

Finally, this book would not have appeared in this form without the extraordinary help and support from Matt Baker, Editor in Chief, International Reading Association.

Introduction

The Teens for Literacy program was launched in 1989 to help inner-city school children improve their reading and writing. The program is a collaborative effort among teachers, students, university educators, and community members. Teachers serve as liaisons between the program and a community partner such as a university, library, or business. Students participate as planners and implementors of rich literacy experiences with peers and younger children. University educators and community members act as resource contacts for the teacher and students or as coordinators of multiple efforts of schools, teachers, and students.

Teens for Literacy was developed for middle school and junior high school students, all of whom are at a turning point in their lives. They are beginning to explore their own identity and place in the world. Participating in the program enables them to consider possibilities of career choices in education, interact constructively with their peers and others, develop pride in their efforts, and appreciate the importance of community service.

Teens for Literacy encourages team members to become involved in promoting literacy in their school and community. Many of these volunteers place a high value on literacy and want to share their own enthusiasm about reading and writing. Teams of four or five students at each school design and participate directly in the literacy process through activities such as

- tutoring peers, elementary children, or adults in reading,
- reading aloud to others,

- coordinating reading contests,
- videotaping literacy events, and
- creating displays or posters to encourage reading.

These activities are carried out under the direction of committed teachers. The activities expose other students to the many rewards that reading and writing provide. In addition to the tutoring and other activities that take place in each school, the teams may visit a nearby university to interact with college students and faculty, or visit a library or local business for mentoring and support. If teens are able to visit a university, they also get a glimpse into the lives of students on campus. If you are not near a college or university, you can easily modify the program to fit your involvement with other community partners.

What to Expect

This book was written because we wanted to share with readers some of the positive and exciting things that have occurred with Teens for Literacy since the beginning of the program. We feel that this is a program that can be started in any school. We intend this book to be a guide for teachers who are interested in promoting literacy in their own school, as well as for others who might want to coordinate this program on a wider scale. We hope that you find this book to be helpful as a model. For us, it is a way to share our stories about a successful literacy-promoting program.

We view the readers of this book as intelligent professionals. You will find an easy-to-follow framework within which you and your students can indulge your creativity. In other words, you will find a great deal of guidance, but we will not tell you that you must "do this" or "do that."

Allen Berger launched the Teens for Literacy program at Miami University in 1989 by speaking with principals of inner-city schools in Cincinnati, Hamilton, and Middletown, Ohio. With the support of Henry Jung, Miami's Director of University Gifts until mid-1998, and numerous graduate assistants, he has directed the program since then. Elizabeth Shafran was a graduate assistant in the master's degree program who helped coordinate the program from 1996 to 1998. We wrote this book jointly. However, some things took place in the early years of the program, such as the development of the program philosophy. Much of this is described in the rest of this Introduction. In describing those years, the pronoun *I* is used to refer to Allen Berger, who shares his creation of the Teens for Literacy program and the foundation on which it is built. Throughout the rest of the book the pronoun *we* is used to represent both our voices.

Our Beliefs

It is our feeling that an honest introduction to a book should include the beliefs of the authors. The following are our beliefs about children and education:

- We believe that children are eager to help other children.

- We believe that many teachers and principals have wonderful ideas.

- We believe that school is an oasis in the lives of many children, thanks to teachers and principals.

- We believe the main difference between children who go to inner-city schools and other children is that inner-city children have less money.

- We believe that parents want to help their children succeed in school.

- We believe children know a lot more than we give them credit for.

Let me elaborate on the last belief. Every time I (Berger) teach a teacher education course, I bring in several teenagers to talk to the undergraduates and graduates enrolled. I try to get a mixture of teens: some from public, parochial, and private schools. There is only one rule for the guests: Do not mention names of teachers, administrators, or anyone else. Why? Because the purpose is to focus on issues, not personalities. For one hour the university students ask the visitors question after question. When the teens leave, my students tend to be in shock: How could these teenagers, some of whom are not even doing well in school, know so much about teaching, learning, and literacy?

The point made by bringing teenagers into a teacher education classroom is that students this age have incredible ideas and, when asked, they can make valuable contributions to improve literacy. We can all learn from the next generation, as can they from us.

Current Status of Education

The Teens for Literacy program on which this book is based began in the Cincinnati, Ohio, area. Following are some recent educational statistics for this region; many of these statistics are the same issues that prompted us to establish a literacy program.

In 1997 the dropout rate was 53% in the Cincinnati Public Schools (Maloney & Buelow, 1997). Among many children of Appalachian background, the dropout rate approaches 100% (Maloney & Buelow, 1997). The teacher-student ratio in Ohio was 36 out of the 50 states in 1997, and the state ranked 50th in the condition of public school buildings, according to the General Accounting Office (Maloney & Buelow, 1997). In 1997 Ohio also ranked 41st in its support of higher education, resulting in a low percentage of children going on to further education. Each geographical area has its own struggles, but these statistics show that literacy is a primary issue in Ohio.

Figure 1 is an article that depicts my own personal experiences in Cincinnati public schools. It is my hope that these insights will help expose others to a more balanced view of public education.

Figure 1

Snapshot of An Inner-City School

By Allen Berger

I spent a couple of hundred hours in two of the toughest inner-city schools in Cincinnati this year. While there, I shadowed, with permission, 7th and 8th grade students from the beginning to the end of school days in September and December. When I wasn't going from class to class with these children, I "hung out" in various classrooms in the schools. I met with individual teachers and with groups of teachers to listen and talk about education.

Here, in a pastiche of images, facts, and impressions, are some of the things I learned.

It was stifling hot on many days in August and September. But at the school I visited then, there was no air conditioning, and many of the windows could not be opened. I sat in on the opening-day meeting with teachers and the principal and listened as the latter set a businesslike tone for the school's operation. After the meeting, teachers spent time getting books and preparing for the arrival of the children the next day.

Throughout that first day, children were told about opportunities and rules. Adults were physically present in hallways and other parts of the school. Between classes, there was no running or loud talking in the halls, which were emptied when the bell rang for the next class. In the classes, students were polite, with an almost even mixture of black and white boys and girls from a variety of backgrounds.

When I shadowed a 7th grade African-American girl in this school, our day began with mathematics. Using an overhead projector, the teacher taught measurement and, later in the semester, angles—acute, obtuse, equilateral, isosceles, and scalene. She ended her classes with time for students to begin their homework, with a little soft music as background. Toward the end of the semester, she had a two-day "Math Olympics."

The second class was reading, where students read and discussed stories from anthologies. (I helped the teacher put covers on the books to protect them.) Later in the semester, they read and listened to, then acted out, a rendition of Charles Dickens' *A Christmas Carol*.

The third class of the day was art, and in December, students were focused on making decorations for a "best holiday classroom door" contest. They were cutting, drawing, and sketching in small groups. One boy talked with me while he drew a good likeness of Ebenezer Scrooge, asking if I had children and where I worked. Toward the end of the class, I helped the teacher make envelopes, so that students could save their work for the next day.

Then came physical education, where students encouraged me to engage in stretching and running activities with them. (The student I was shadowing did 60 pushups, according to a progress chart.) During transitions from one activity to another, some of the others practiced back handsprings, cartwheels, double-rope jumping, and basketball.

At fifth-period lunch, I talked and ate with several teachers who belonged to what is called "The Dream Team." These five core-academic teachers, together with the "inclusion" teacher, meet every day to plan engaging activities for the students. On the basis of what they call "the three A's"—academics, attendance, and attitude—the Dream Team treats six "students of the month" (and, on one occasion, me) to brunch at a nearby restaurant.

Back in sixth-period social studies, the students paged through atlases to examine maps of Iraq (then in the news) and other countries, including the United States. On other days, they completed assignments relating to the dictionary, current events, and the U.S. Constitution.

In science class, students took part in a variety of hands-on activities relating to measurement and the classification of objects such as cylinders, cubes, diamonds, boxes, squares, rectangles, and columns. Their homework included finding articles on science in newspapers and magazines.

The last class of the day was English. Working in semicircles, students revised autobiographies they had written earlier. They also studied the kinds of sentences—declarative, interrogative, imperative, and exclamatory—for their homework assignment. On other days, they discussed concrete and sensory details in paragraphs.

(continued)

Figure 1 (continued)

What else did I learn in this school, whose parking-lot entrance requires knowledge of a four-digit code in order for the school door to open? I learned that the children work in classrooms where most of the clocks don't work. Where many of the chairs and desks are broken. Where most of the books and materials are old and worn. Where only a handful of out-of-date computers are available in the library and a few other rooms. Where the wiring may not be up to date enough to support many more computers. Where paint is peeling and ceilings look water-damaged.

I learned also about parents who want the best for their children. One such parent came to a meeting of the Dream Team I attended. She was eager to get the teacher's side of her child's story. Each team member took three minutes to explain that student's absences, tardiness, missing homework. The parent was stunned. She and the teachers then considered concrete ways to help her daughter focus on school.

After the parent left, another student came in. She had been invited because the team was concerned about her and, in succession, each team member talked to her about homework, absences, tardinesses. They asked the girl how they could help her more in school and offered to tutor her after school—even adding that, if she missed the bus because of this, they would drive her home. I was told these meetings with students and parents took place weekly.

But I also learned about other kinds of adults in these children's lives: About a child who was stabbed by her mother 18 times one weekend. About a girl who told me she goes to sleep after midnight every night because of the fierce noise outside her windows—"drug selling and gunshots," she said. About a boy who was being sexually attacked by bullies as he went to and from school and landed in a hospital. After school one day, a teacher took him get-well cards that his classmates had created.

For many children, I learned, an inner-city school is an oasis. They come to a school that is clean, neat, and orderly. They have teachers with high expectations of them. On blackboards and bulletin boards they read a barrage of messages on values: *Study Smarter. Go For It! Make the World a Better Place. Be Cheerful. Spread Sunshine Everyday. Save a Space for Rainbows and Dreams. Studying Can Make It Happen. If You Believe It, You Can Achieve It. Everyone Smiles in the Same Language.*

They see parent-volunteers helping in a newly painted parent center at the school. Several times each day, they hear the principal reminding them to give "110 percent effort." They feel the warmth from teachers who give hugs and home phone numbers to students who have to transfer to other schools because of circumstances beyond their control.

I observed the goodwill, decency, and humor of children and teachers working in a building with rooms that are stifling in September and freezing in December. It was so cold one winter day that my hands were shaking as I turned the pages of an encyclopedia while students completed an assignment on biographies in the school library. Everyone was wearing coats. The wind blew in around the doors and windows. It was even worse in the art room. There, I actually shivered, and many of the students, some mumbling under their breath about the cold, wore hats and coats while painting and washing their hands in freezing water.

The U.S. General Accounting Office has reported that public school buildings in Ohio are in the worst condition of all the schools in the United States.

On my last day—after Hanukkah and before Christmas and Kwanzaa—I stopped in to say good-bye and thank the principal. Though he has an open-door policy and regularly visits all parts of the school, at that moment he was in a meeting in his office with the door closed. So I wrote a note for him and left it with someone at the front office. Then I walked outside to a cold but bright winter day. The sun was shining, even though snow was beginning to fall.

Reprinted with permission from *Education Week, 16*(27), April 9, 1997.

It is because of such adverse conditions and minimal support for public education that I felt a program with the goals and ideas of Teens for Literacy would be beneficial to children, teachers, and administrators. Despite what may be happening with the physical condition of schools, there are many positive aspects of schooling that I thought that Teens for Literacy could build on, especially the enthusiasm and dedication of teachers and students.

Organization of the Book

This book is organized to guide readers through the stages of implementing and carrying out the program. Chapter One is an example of the Teens for Literacy program in action; written as a narrative, this chapter describes the program in two inner-city middle schools. Chapter Two explains the main objectives of the program, outlines the key components, explains the tutoring element of the program, and describes activities that can be done as part of the program. Chapter Three offers guidelines for setting up the program at an individual school, and includes a sample proposal that can be used to request funding for the program. Because so many students in the program choose to focus on tutoring, we have devoted Chapter Four to this topic. This chapter offers suggestions on establishing tutoring goals, choosing tutors and pairing them with tutees, and structuring a tutoring lesson. Chapter Five offers information on the teens' visits to a local university; this experience exposes students to educational opportunities beyond high school. If you want to expand the program beyond an individual school to other schools in a district, ways to do this are discussed in Chapter Six. Chapter Seven focuses on how to evaluate the program's success and how to spread the word about the benefits of Teens for Literacy. We conclude the book with an Appendix that includes lists of resources that will be useful to you as you implement the program in your school or district.

As you progress through this book, you will gain an enormous sense of satisfaction as you consider ways to implement many of these ideas in your school or district.

Chapter One

Snapshot of Teens for Literacy

The first bell rings, signaling the beginning of another school day. The typical signs of a middle school culture are all around: clanging lockers, posters of school rules paired with an advertisement for a school dance, and students dashing to class carrying spiral-bound notebooks covered in doodles. The halls soon clear as the tardy bell rings.

A classroom door is covered with enthusiastic hand-drawn signs exclaiming the benefits of reading. It is the classroom of Mrs. Vincent, a language arts teacher. She is in the midst of welcoming students and explaining their first assignment of the morning. The students seem comfortable in this morning routine. They sharpen their pencils, borrow notebook paper from one another, and begin the task of copying definitions from the chalkboard. Some students in Mrs. Vincent's class are Teens for Literacy members, student volunteers who have chosen to work within their schools and communities to promote literacy.

Most of these students have been struggling with passing the eighth-grade proficiency test. This test is an assessment tool mandated by the State of Ohio to determine if students are meeting basic requirements at set grade levels. The students do not seem overly concerned with all the testing as they continue to copy the definitions from the board in preparation for writing a persuasive essay. One student reminds another that they have a Teens for Literacy meeting during third period in Mrs. Phillips's room.

Several students straggle into Mrs. Phillips's room finishing conversations with friends. The Teens for Literacy group consists of six seventh-grade students, three girls and three boys. Two of the students are African American and the other four are white. As soon as they spot their teacher, the students bombard her with questions about an event they are planning. She instructs them to sit in a circle of chairs, and the meeting begins. The Teens for Literacy members are in the midst of planning some of the activities that they will do with their tutees during the school year. They review what has been done in years past and comment on what they liked or did not like. Eventually it is decided that at the end of the fall, they will take their tutees to a local pumpkin patch. Mrs. Phillips asks them how they can relate this to literacy. A slew of ideas pour from the students: writing stories about the pumpkin patch, reading books about farms, and labeling photos taken during the field trip.

This Teens for Literacy team tutors kindergartners who are in an elementary school that is in the same building as the middle school. Once a week, during class or after school, the tutors walk to the kindergartners' classroom to read aloud to the children and tutor them in reading. The way these middle school students are talking about the kindergartners shows that they have a great deal of affection for them. It is only the first month of the school year.

Mrs. Phillips has been teacher-liaison of her school's Teens for Literacy team for 8 years, and she is an enthusiastic supporter of the program. Over the years she has observed how the relationship becomes mutually beneficial for the adolescents and the children. The middle school students learn a strong sense of responsibility and commitment to their tutees. The experience of reading aloud to the children renews an excitement about reading. She knows this because the team meets after the tutoring session to discuss their teaching experience. This is another positive character-building aspect of Mrs. Phillips's program; the teens learn how to collaborate in a professional-type meeting situation. Mrs. Phillips also observes how the students become careful listeners and learn to respect one another as a result.

The kindergarten students also benefit from many elements of the program, such as the read-aloud activities. The middle school students interact with the children, pointing out different letters, numbers, and colors in the books. Additionally, the tutors attempt to guide an understanding of literary techniques such as plot, character, humor, and tone. The kindergarten teacher stresses how much the children look up to the teens. She praises the Teens for Literacy tutors for acting as such wonderful role models.

In years past the tutors and tutees have taken field trips together as a part of Teens for Literacy. Typically, in early December, the middle school teacher reads a children's storybook version of *The Nutcracker* to the kindergartners. The next week each middle school student is paired with a kindergarten child and, with the help of six chaperones, they all walk a few blocks to see a performance of *The Nutcracker* ballet. In this example the teacher-liaison was able to integrate an artistic and cultural experience with a literacy event.

The sense of community that is produced as a result of the Teens for Literacy program is commended by both the middle school teacher and the kindergarten teacher. The teachers relate how vital these feelings of security are in urban schools that lack appropriate materials and funds. Some of the Teens for Literacy funds that are provided by alumni at a local university have been used to purchase an accelerated reader program for the computer in Mrs. Phillips's classroom. In this particular inner-city school, there are currently no computers connected to the Internet. Mrs. Phillips feels grateful to have the chance to integrate technology into her classroom in a productive way. She cites this computer program as an extremely efficient educational source. The teens compete, not with one another, but on an individual basis for material rewards. Occasionally, there are pizza parties given for those who have accumulated a certain number of points.

Mrs. Phillips is proud to be involved with a program that allows her students to spend time on service to their community. She applauds her students for working hard and is happy to see how they enjoy spending time promoting literacy and building friendships.

Less than 5 miles from the middle school at which Mrs. Phillips teaches is another inner-city middle school. Like many other inner-city schools, the building is in the middle of several apartment complexes. Outside the school in the late afternoon, one can see children hanging out on porch stoops or walking to the local convenience store. The school is surrounded by a chain-link fence that serves as the barrier between the street and the schoolyard blacktop. There are a few basketball hoops that are used for after-school and weekend games by children in the neighborhood.

School has been dismissed for 15 minutes, so the hallways are almost deserted except for an occasional teacher walking between classrooms. On the second floor is Ms. Hart's classroom. This is the first meeting for this Teens for Literacy team at this middle school. As Teens for Literacy students at Mrs. Phillips's school are reviewing activities that have been done in past years, Ms. Hart and her seventh graders are brainstorming what they envision their newly formed Teens for Literacy team could be. They know the basic structure of the program: A teacher at a middle school serves as a coordinator for a local Teens for Literacy team. The team is made up of the teacher and a group of volunteer middle school students. The goal of this team is to serve its school and community by promoting literacy locally. Because each community is different, each team designs and implements these literacy activities uniquely.

At this first meeting of the team there are three boys and one girl, all African American, and Ms. Hart. She has talked to a few other Teens for Literacy teams that have participated in the program for several years. She shares some of the background information with the rest of the team about activities that have been successful at other schools, such as a read-a-thon, acting in plays for younger students, and creating posters for the school encouraging students to read for fun. This team already has agreed that they would like to tutor younger students at an elementary school that is one block from their school. They begin to discuss how some of the activities that other schools have done would work with the students at the elementary school.

Ms. Hart challenges the students to think of other things that would be original to their Teens for Literacy team. One boy mentions that it would be good to get adults in the community involved in literacy events as well. He suggests having a picnic in the spring that would be open to anyone who lived near the school. The other team members seem to like this idea, so Ms. Hart encourages them to pursue it.

One of the boys mentions that he needs to leave to catch the next bus. At this school, many of the students ride the city bus back and forth to school because there is no school transportation system. Ms. Hart quickly reads back to the students some of the literacy ideas that they have brainstormed in the meeting. They set the next meeting time for next week, again after school. The students say their goodbyes to one another and go their separate ways. A new Teens for Literacy team is well on its way.

Chapter Two

Objectives and Components of Teens for Literacy

Main Objectives of the Program

There are three main objectives that form the basis for Teens for Literacy. The first is to involve students directly in promoting literacy or making others aware of literacy issues. In doing so, students take an active role in shaping their education and influencing others' educational experiences. They are able to demonstrate that they value literacy as an important part of their lives. One teacher in our program recognized this as he watched fifth- and sixth-grade members of his Teens for Literacy team reading aloud to their tutees. As the members were lying on their stomachs on a carpet sharing a story, the younger children cuddled up to them and looked at them admiringly like a big brother or sister. No one watching this would have guessed that these fifth- and sixth-grade students had been labeled as dysfunctional readers or behavior problems. To the younger children they were good readers who helped teach them.

The second objective is to encourage the middle school or junior high school students to continue their learning at a postsecondary educational institution. Some students who participate in the program do not see college as a realistic option. We hope that the success that they feel as tutors helps motivate them to be lifelong learners. Years after students have been in Teens for Literacy, we phone or write to them. Most students have continued their formal education after high school by attending a university or vocational school. It is exciting to hear of and from students who have earned scholarships to colleges and universities. One such student, who wrote in her scholarship application essay about her participation in Teens for Literacy, was awarded a full scholarship to a prestigious university.

The third objective—helping acquaint students with teaching as a possible career—was not initially included in the goals of the program. It developed with the inclusion of Shadowing Day (see Chapter Five for a thorough discussion of this activity). When the visiting students spend the whole day shadowing undergraduates who are majoring in education, they gain a greater understanding of what it takes to become a teacher. They participate in university courses focusing on teaching and they have conversations with the students in these classes. They learn the importance of tutoring and other volunteer activities. Through their own tutoring and other activities, they begin to develop confidence in their ability to help others. Many join Teens for Literacy with experience babysitting or playing and working with younger siblings, but these teens do not consider teaching as a future profession until after their involvement in the program.

There are many other related outcomes for students who participate in Teens for Literacy. The most noticeable is the development of leadership abilities. By being a tutor each teen guides others in improving reading and writing. When students see they are actually helping other students, their confidence increases. Years later, when students who have been in the program are contacted, they tell how Teens for Literacy helped them understand what it takes to be a leader.

By helping others in their schools and neighborhoods, students begin to understand how they fit into their own communities. They see their work having an impact. This is powerful: It makes them reflect on their ability to make a difference in the world beginning with one person.

Key Components

There are two key components to the Teens for Literacy program. The first is the tutoring and other activities that occur at each school.

This is the time that the school team members, the volunteer students, work to improve literacy in their own schools and community. What occurs at each school is self-directed by the school team based on the needs of the school and its community.

Throughout the span of a school year a Teens for Literacy team engages in many activities. In every school each member tutors one or more students once a week; these tutees can be peers in the middle schools or children at a nearby elementary school. Who, what, where, and when is decided by each team at the beginning of the school year. These teams also plan literacy events or activities in which they will participate over the year.

The second component of Teens for Literacy is visits by each school team to a nearby community partner such as a university, library, or business. In our situation, we chose to collaborate with a local university. Five times throughout the year all the school teams drive to the university to participate in a wide variety of activities encouraging the members to continue their education after high school. We structure these five sessions to meet the needs of our Teens for Literacy program: Orientation session (visit 1), World Wide Web workshop (visit 2), tour of the university broadcasting facility (visit 3), Shadowing Day (visit 4), and the recognition luncheon (visit 5). We also include walking through a dormitory, visiting the university art museum, taking a tour of the recreation facility, and touring the campus. These visits are also an opportunity to support each member's own growth in literacy development by discussing what activities are happening locally at each school and through sharing ideas on how to improve these activities, particularly tutoring.

Although the original Teens for Literacy program is a collaborative effort between local schools and a university, the program can be adapted to other community partners. It is vital to establish a connection between the Teens for Literacy student volunteers and a mentoring group. This mentoring group serves students as an additional training resource for students on tutoring and a source for encouragement and inspiration for their efforts.

A local library can be an excellent collaborative community resource. Librarians work with people to help them with their literacy needs. They are knowledgeable in how to interest reluctant readers and make them feel comfortable in selecting books that are at an appropriate reading level. These are skills that the Teens for Literacy student volunteers need to develop with the students they tutor. The team members could then use the library as a physical location to provide tutoring or to participate in a weekend read-aloud event. By working with a library, the Teens for Literacy program is expanding its scope into the community.

Many businesses are also willing to participate in a mentoring role toward a literacy-promoting group such as a Teens for Literacy team. Businesses see this as a way to provide community service, and it can be used to further develop the overall educational skill level in the area where they are located. Businesses also could provide some technology training to students to help them become proficient in using the World Wide Web, which could then be incorporated into a tutoring session. Teens for Literacy team members could shadow employees to see how important literacy is in a person's life. Most importantly, the connection that some of the members may develop with the business employees could encourage them to continue with their education beyond a high school degree.

To help you get a better feel for Teens for Literacy, the following section offers examples of actual tutoring formats and literacy activities that schools are doing and have done.

Tutoring

What goes on in the schools varies with the initiative and imagination of the students. Tutoring is one activity in which every school team participates. How this plays out in each school differs. In one school the tutoring is in the same building as another school; Teens for Literacy middle school students walk down the corridor into the elementary school. For many years these team members tutored first-grade students, and now they are tutoring fourth-grade students. Once a week team members read to the younger students, and the younger students read to the older teens. (See Chapter 4 for strategies for implementing the tutoring component of the program.)

In another school the teens in the program tutor developmentally disabled children several times each week. These team members and their tutees develop a close relationship. They know each other's reading and writing interests and personal interests. In other schools many teens also tutor children their own age who need help in reading and writing, test taking, and study skills. The tutoring goes on inside classrooms, in hallways, and at all times of the day. Lately, some tutoring has focused on preparing peers for statewide proficiency tests.

What happens during the tutoring sessions differs in each school. Some members read books that the tutees are interested in such as school library books checked out that week. Some children have a favorite book that they want read to them time and again. Many members have remarked how they often remember books they are reading to the younger students from when they were that age.

Some teams develop a big brother/big sister reading program (unconnected to the organization of that name) in which students of different ages read to each other. Sometimes the tutor and the tutee "buddy read." In buddy reading, the tutor or the tutee will pick a book that both can read. Then, one person will read one page, and the other person will read the next. This continues until the book is completed. This is a powerful interaction to observe and sparks discussion about the story and the students' own personal experiences. The experience of having two voices read the book aloud makes the story come alive. They can hear themselves read but they also know that someone else is helping them create the story.

Most of the tutoring sessions make the reading and writing connection for students. The tutor and the tutee may read a book together and then the tutee writes about the story. Sometimes only the tutee reads a book to focus on a specific skill. The tutee's teacher informs the tutor of this before the session. After the tutee has read the book, there may be an accompanying activity sheet that involves writing about the story. In some cases the reading and writing are not related, but both might occur during a tutoring session. This is especially true when team members are tutoring older students such as their peers. In one junior high school with a Teens for Literacy program, the focus of the tutoring sessions is on the state proficiency test that is given near the end of the school year. The members tutor classmates on the reading passages or how to write a good essay for the writing portion of the test. This learning is purposeful to the students in a way that is different from working on general literacy skills.

More Program Activities

The creativity of the Teens for Literacy team members is demonstrated by their development and implementation of activities in addition to tutoring. Most of the time this decision-making process is led by the teacher-liaison. What the students decide to do varies with their school's and community's needs. One school decided to design a billboard showing the importance of reading. It was effective in a community that is centered around an industrial plant, because the billboard was placed near the plant so that people driving to and from work saw it every day.

We always wait with anticipation for one of our school teams to announce their school's spring literacy assembly, an annual event planned by this particular school. Usually, the team challenges all the students in grades 7 and 8 to read as much as they can. The students read a certain amount, either in number of pages or in duration of time. Each time they complete a designated amount, they place one card with their name on it in a box. The highlight event of the assembly is when a team member or teacher-liaison draws students' names from the box and the students are recognized in front of their peers. We discovered when we talked to the winning students after the literacy assembly that they achieved a great deal of personal satisfaction from the books they read, and that the events at the literacy assembly were just "frosting on the cake."

The teens also read with residents of a local senior citizens' home. Other team members develop videos promoting literacy, and some promote books and authors over the school public address system. In school corridors they display posters of famous athletes and other personalities supporting literacy. Other teams have 1,000-minute reading clubs through which students get a prize for reading 1,000 minutes over a given period of time.

These are representative examples of what students and teachers do to improve literacy through their schools and community. As we have shown, there are a variety of approaches to tutoring and activities by each school team. What has been done in one school can be replicated easily in other schools.

We have given you the basic framework of the Teens for Literacy program and several examples of how it can be adapted to a school. The next chapter contains more practical ideas to use in implementing a program in your school.

Chapter Three

Planning the Program at an Individual School

In this chapter you will find steps for setting up a Teens for Literacy team in your school. This is presented in chronological order over the span of an academic year to give a better understanding of the various components of the program. Several events that are described occur repeatedly throughout the year such as tutoring, planning events, and implementing activities. The time line that follows can be adjusted to fit your own schedule.

Time Line

Following is a brief outline of some of the major elements of the program:

Early September

If your Teens for Literacy program is coordinated with a university or community partner, here are the typical steps:

- The teacher-liaison(s) is selected.
- Team members are selected by the teacher-liaison.
- The first school team meeting is held during which goals are proposed for the school year.

- School teams are told about the first visit (orientation visit) to their partner (for example, a university or business).
- Other school activities are considered.

The five visits to a community partner follow:

Late September or Early October

- The first meeting (orientation session) is held to introduce the program and provide tutoring tips. If there is more than one team, all meet together for the orientation session.
- Tutoring and activities in each school begin on a full-time basis.

November

- The second meeting—the World Wide Web workshop—is held with other school teams.

February

- The third meeting is a guided tour of a broadcasting facility.

March

- The fourth meeting with the school teams is to participate with a business, school, or university in Shadowing Day.

Late April/Early May

- The fifth meeting is held with community partner at a luncheon recognition banquet. This involves administrators, community members, and program supporters.

Member Selection

One role that needs to be defined is that of a team member. This is the title given to the middle school or junior high school student who is a part of the Teens for Literacy program. The title is important because it reflects the student's decision to participate in the program. It also implies that each person is part of a larger group, Teens for Literacy, and all members play an important role in promoting literacy.

Once the teacher-liaison has been selected or has chosen to initiate the program (the teacher-liaison selection process is discussed in Chapter Six), the next step is to decide which students will participate in the program. The teams consist of four or five members. This small group size should be encouraged because it is easier to develop the program with just a few people. In some schools there are more students who take part in the tutoring and activities than just the members. Sometimes there are as many as 20 additional students per school who tutor on a regular basis who are not members. In this situation it is the four or five members and the teacher-liaison who make up the decision-making team. When the program has been established long enough in your school and the teacher-liaisons and administrators are comfortable with it, you may decide to increase the number of team members.

It is the responsibility of the teacher-liaison to select the members. Ideally, this occurs within the first few weeks of the school year, enabling the whole team to participate in the first visit to a university or community partner in late September or early October. In some schools there are waiting lists of interested students compiled at the end of the previous school year.

There are many ways to select students for the teams. You may choose to select only members from your own classes because of your trust for and familiarity with those students. However, this selection process should not be completely informal; you may ask each interested student to write an essay about a designated topic. The teacher-liaison should look for students who are responsible, resourceful, and motivated. On a more practical note, the students should have a study hall period to use for tutoring.

Some teacher-liaisons take a different approach. You might choose students you think might benefit from behavior modification. These students range in their reading ability levels. The teacher's goal is to have the students who are slower in the reading process develop into capable students who can say, "I'm a teacher." The teacher liaison also should pay attention to gender and racial balances when selecting team members.

Sometimes the selection process of the members is less formal and more intuitive. Several years ago one of the local team teachers was at a fair put on by a local church. She saw a girl who was painting the faces of some younger children. As the teacher watched the girl interact with the children, she recognized that the girl was an ideal candidate for a Teens for Literacy team member. The teacher approached the girl and told her that when she got to the junior high school she should consider joining the Teens for Literacy program. The girl eventually became one of the five Teens for Literacy members at her junior high school.

As mentioned, most of the teacher-liaisons are language arts or reading teachers. This is a great advantage in determining who would work well in the program because the teachers have first-hand knowledge of a student's abilities and attitude toward literacy and are able to select team members. A second option is to seek recommendations from other teachers in the schools. The selection process for each team might differ according to the teacher's decision. This tends to result in a very diverse Teens for Literacy school team. A third option is to have an open selection process schoolwide using interviews and questionnaires for all interested students. We have found that all three ways are successful.

There is no model for what an ideal Teens for Literacy member is, but there are two main criteria. The first is that the student should demonstrate a high level of competency in literacy-based skills. The rationale for this is that the members will have a well-developed knowledge base for tutoring others. The second is to choose tutors who are enthusiastic about tutoring and other learning activities. They may not be the best students in the class, but they will be dedicated to the goals of the program and have an enthusiastic outlook

on literacy that might carry over to those with whom they are working. The belief is that, by tutoring, these students will further develop their own skills. You may find that the latter approach is the more
appropriate one to take. It is hard to beat enthusiasm.

Another consideration when selecting students is their ability and
willingness to participate in after-school meetings, if this is the
agreed-on meeting time. And keep in mind the students' transportation situations. A later bus may not be available in some schools, particularly when students must rely on public transportation. For one
teacher, about half the students in her program are bused across town.
When the team visits the nearby university, they do not get back in
time for the bus so she drives some of the students to their homes.
She cannot, however, do this for everyone; some of her team members need to be within walking distance of the school. Additionally,
some students have after-school activities already. Bring up these
issues with potential members before they make a commitment to the
program.

Ironing Out the Details

Details that need to be worked out include how the Teens for
Literacy program fits into your school structure. Because most of the
program activities that the students participate in occur during the
school day, it would not be accurate to call Teens for Literacy a club,
which usually meets after school. Teens for Literacy might be called
an extracurricular activity or a service organization. The program
might be considered part of the language arts or reading class. Sometimes the program is tied directly to the teacher-liaison; that is, it is
known as "so and so's" program. There is no single answer—or
rather, the answer depends on your school. Regardless of what you
call the program, it is important for the team to meet on a regular
basis for tutoring and other activities to occur steadily and system-
atically.

Another issue is the degree of supervision that the teacher-liaison
will have with the members. As mentioned, there are instances in

which members may walk a few blocks between schools. Whether or not you choose to walk with the students or transport them depends on many factors, a major one being school policy. Some school and districts have rules that determine whether or not it is necessary for a teacher-liaison to accompany the students. Such rules may stem from the environment in which the school is located, events in the past, parental concerns, or insurance policies.

Teacher-liaisons may not be able to accompany the members to the tutoring sessions because of their own teaching schedules, so it may be necessary to find another responsible adult to accompany the students, if a high degree of supervision is required. A more ambiguous factor that plays into the level of supervision is the degree to which the teacher-liaison knows and trusts the students. In one school the teacher-liaison has had her members as students for more than 2 years, and had developed a rapport with them prior to their being her students. The teacher-liaison has a high degree of trust in the team members. In return they honor this relationship by not violating any rules or regulations. However, this is not the situation in all schools.

The administrator may decide that the teacher-liaison will accompany team members during school time to and from the community partner. Because of this, alternative arrangements may need to be made regarding the teacher-liaison's teaching schedule. Usually, this is resolved through the cooperation of other teachers in the building who during their planning periods or lunch time volunteer to substitute for the teacher liaison's class. This demonstrates the strong support within a school for the Teens for Literacy program. However, you may need to visit the community partner after school hours. Related to visits to the community partner is the physical transportation of the members. Usually this is done by the teacher-liaisons in their personal cars or in a rented vehicle. Again, check district or school policy.

The ongoing relationship with each school principal is essential to building a network of support for the program. By keeping the lines of communication open, the program is on its way to success in your school.

First Team Meeting

The first in-school meeting of the Teens for Literacy team usually occurs early in the school year. The primary purpose is to set the foundation for the rest of the year by planning the structure of the tutoring sessions and other literacy activities. Because each school has a different way to promote literacy in its community, there is not a specific framework that the school must work within. This is one of the unique aspects of Teens for Literacy. It enables each school to be creative in meeting its needs. As a result, one school may decide to focus its tutoring on peers because of lower state proficiency test scores in reading and writing. Another school may choose to work with fourth graders at a nearby elementary school.

The first order of business is to create the vision of the Teens for Literacy team for the year. This entails identifying what the needs of the school and community are, the people, and how their needs will be met. Teams engage in cooperative brainstorming with the members and teacher-liaison giving suggestions. This experience is effective for the members because they create their own plan for the year rather than follow someone else's format. The teacher-liaison is both a contributor and facilitator.

At this point the school team decides who they will tutor. There are many possibilities: elementary school students, peers who are below the appropriate skill level, students mentally challenged, or adults in the community. You should consider the proximity of tutees to the school, the degree of support from the students' teachers, and the frequency that the tutees are available to be tutored. The members should not be placed in a situation in which they feel uncomfortable with the tutees they are tutoring. That is, if team members do not feel qualified to tutor a specific population, such as adults, then choose another group.

The school team should plan where and when the weekly tutoring session will occur. Usually, it takes place in the tutee's classroom when the tutor has a free period. For some this means a study hall period from which they are excused. In one school the tutors' schedules did not have any open periods, so the members decided to tutor during their lunch period. Some tutoring also goes on early in the morning at what might be called a breakfast reading club.

The other major undertaking for the first school team meeting is to create an outline of activities the team will design and participate in for the year. The activities that are selected should match the specific goals of each school. For example, if Teens for Literacy members at a junior high school identify students in their own grades needing support because of a lack of interest in reading, most of the activities would focus on getting students excited about reading. Such activities might include holding a book fair, putting on a book-a-thon, having a class read-in, or connecting reading with sports. The school team could come up with a sketch of how the activities will take place during the year.

The degree to which the teacher-liaison makes decisions for the group varies with each school team. You may find that the dynamics of each team really alter the amount of decision making that you do for that year. There are always some regular activities that the school team will participate in, one being tutoring. However, beyond that it is the team's creation. What results are different approaches to promoting literacy. For example, a school team decided to write and publish a Teens for Literacy newsletter because of their interest in writing. The next year a different team chose to concentrate on developing state proficiency-test intervention for their classmates. This flexibility in decision making enables each team to assess its community's needs each year and adjust its activities accordingly. For the teacher, though, it translates into a lot of coordination. There might be several ideas by the members that are not realistic in the school setting, either because of funding, school policy, material resources, or simply the lack of people available to help carry out the event. This is where you step in with suggestions.

The teacher-liaison and members need to have a regular meeting time to plan activities, talk about tutoring, and give feedback on progress. Meeting at least once a week enables the team to maintain sufficient contact for productive communication. In addition to planning events these meetings give the teacher-liaison an opportunity to update the members on rules or regulations that may affect them, such as school policy on behavior on field trips. At this initial meeting it is imperative to make members aware of the school policy as it affects Teens for Literacy.

In our program we provide each school with a yearly planning form so each team can record its goals and activities for the school year. It is a helpful way to document some of the logistical details and provide an idea where the school team is focusing its energy. This form is handed in at the first meeting, the orientation session for all the teams. Most schools like to come back to the form at the end of the school year to compare the outcomes with the goals that were outlined in the beginning of the year.

Funding

Uses of Funding

Funding is not inherently essential to a Teens for Literacy program, but it is certainly helpful. You could spend $1,500 for each school as follows: $500 for the teacher-liaison, $500 for curricular materials, and $500 to divide among the student volunteers, with each receiving $5 for each month of participation in the program. The teacher-liaison would use his or her compensation to pay for travel to and from the university. If there are coteacher-liaisons for a school, they equally divide the $500. Each participating school receives $500 for the team to purchase materials such as books, word games, or software.

The books that are purchased come from a variety of sources and are read by different people. Paperback books from book fairs such as Scholastic Book Club, Pages Book Fair, and Troll Book Fair are very popular (see the Appendix for contact information for these companies.) One school plans and holds a schoolwide biannual book fair. The book fair company they work with enables the school to buy additional books at a discounted rate from the profits they make from the fair. Consequently, for each book fair they hold, they have been able to donate about $100 worth of books to each reading classroom in the school. Additionally, one of the Teens for Literacy members suggested that books be donated to a local shelter for needy children. The shelter greatly appreciates the books and the members enjoy being able to contribute to their community. Other times books are used as incentives for the tutors and the tutees. Sometimes the students go to the local bookstore during a lunch period and pick out a favorite book for themselves. Pop-up books from National Geographic are a favorite among many middle school students.

One of the most common uses of funding for supplies is to purchase skill-building materials such as workbooks, posters, or textbooks for the tutees. These help to provide a framework for the tutors as they work with their tutees. Most are ordered from educational catalogs or purchased directly at education supply stores. (Although workbooks may be frowned on by some educators, many children like the structure and sense of progress; they also can serve as a jumping off point for their own ideas and activities.) Paperback dictionaries and thesauruses also are used widely.

Junior Great Books is another literacy resource that is being integrated into classrooms. These books are compilations of stories for a variety of reading levels. They are being used in small groups to meet the needs of a variety of readers. These books are a good tool for getting literacy in the classroom when resources are limited and the stories serve as good discussion starters. (Information about these books and software is in the Appendix.)

A popular resource purchase in recent years has been the Accelerated Reader computer software program. This program has questions that relate to hundreds of books. When students finish a book, they can answer questions about the book on the computer. Their score is converted into a point system, which is then used as a basis for earning incentives, such as a copy of the book they read. In the schools where the software is being used the teacher-liaisons and teachers of the tutees have seen a dramatic increase in the number of books read by students. A seventh-grade student in a nearby school completed 16 chapter books in 6 months. For her and many others this has become a way to enjoy reading good literature while getting immediate feedback on story comprehension.

Some of the supply money also is used in simple, creative ways to encourage parental involvement in Teens for Literacy. One teacher uses part of the money for letters to be sent home. Each letter provides an update on what the child has been doing while being tutored and how he or she is progressing. What is really captivating is the use of stationery with a photograph of the tutee with his or her tutor so the parents or guardians are introduced to the student tutoring their child. This particular teacher found this to be an extremely effective means of establishing parental support and involvement in Teens for Literacy.

Inexpensive cameras and film can be used innovatively. Photos have been taken to document the events that the school team has participated in through the year. At the end of the school year the photos are displayed on posters and in slide shows at the Teens for Literacy recognition luncheon. (See the Teens for Literacy Web site— www.muohio.edu/~bergera/teensforliteracy—for samples of these photos.) Photos taken of unusual objects or everyday activities also serve as story starters for the tutees during their tutoring sessions.

Some teacher-liaisons and their teams choose to use the supply money for materials or events that might not be directly related to promoting literacy but which benefit students in other ways. For example, at one school the tutoring takes place with students the same age as the tutors: The tutees are developmentally handicapped students who are usually included in some classes throughout the day. Both the teacher-liaison and the tutees' teachers have identified socialization as one of the main needs of these tutees. Consequently, some of the supply money for that school team is spent for a few pizza parties during the year. For many tutees, this is the first time they really feel involved in their school.

Finally, each student can be paid $5 for each month that he or she is on a team. Although one can argue the pros and cons of paying students, the small sum is not their incentive, for most do not even know about it until they receive their checks. We pay them because we think they deserve it.

Sources of Funding

Where does the funding come from? Interested alumni at a university or business that has literacy-promoting interests can be invited to support the program. Individuals may contribute a thousand or more dollars each year. Sometimes their contribution is matched by a company or corporation. Here are some ways that you might try to obtain money:

- Talk to the person in charge of gifts at a university, and tell him or her about Teens for Literacy.

- Talk to someone in a company or corporation; if the organization sponsors a sports team, perhaps they will sponsor Teens for Literacy.

- Talk to your Parent-Teacher Association or Organization. They may be delighted to sponsor Teens for Literacy in your school.

- Check your local and state literacy organizations. Many have money available for programs to improve literacy. Do not let the thought of competition dissuade you.

- Do not overlook major national and international professional organizations such as the International Reading Association (IRA) and the National Council of Teachers of English (NCTE). Call and ask for information relating to funding programs to improve literacy.

- Finally, although there is not as much funding available for literacy as there is for math and science, there is still money available. Talk to a grant writer (if there is one) in your school district, or check library books containing information about sources of funding for literacy improvement. Some of these sources might be businesses, corporations, or your state or federal government.

The sample proposal on the next page was submitted to a variety of organizations to seek funding for Teens for Literacy. It provides a general framework for how to structure your funding requests.

The Problem: Inner-city students score well below average on state and national tests. They also have a smaller chance to go on to college. The dropout rate is now 53% in Cincinnati Public Schools. Among many children of Appalachian background, the dropout rate approaches 100%. We cannot permit this pattern to continue.

The Solution: Teens for Literacy is a program that will help inner-city students improve their test scores and will encourage them to seek higher education. I began the program in 1989, and we have traced many of the children who have been in the program during the early years. They have praised the program and cited it as having contributed to their success in college and in the workplace.

Plan of Action: With the help of the school principal, teams of teens in middle schools and junior high schools will be formed. These teams will focus on ways to improve literacy in their schools and neighborhoods. They will also make periodic visits to the campus of a local university to learn about campus life.

Implementation: We propose to form teams in 10 inner-city schools in southwest Ohio for the 1999-2000 academic year. These teams will be composed of students of varying backgrounds. With the guidance of a teacher, they will investigate and implement ways that they have decided on to improve literacy. They may choose to do tutoring, have 1,000-minute reading clubs, develop audio- and videotapes encouraging reading and writing, to name a few examples. The tutoring they do will be based on suggested exercises found in Ohio's *Model Competency-Based Language Arts Program*. The exercises have a direct connection to the Ohio Proficiency Tests.

Once the five-person teams are formed, they will gain additional ideas during their visits to a local university and have the opportunity to experience the college environment. During their first visit, they will meet with college students who tutor in the Office of Learning Assistance to gain practical, useful tips for tutoring. Four more visits will take place during the school year. In November, the students will go to a radio or television studio. In February, they will develop additional computer-related skills. In March, they will shadow undergraduates for a day, going to classes, to lunch, and walking the campus together. The program will conclude in late April with a luncheon during which students share their ideas with the other students, teachers, and principals assembled.

Evaluation: Students in the program will be compared with other students in their own schools in regard to their success in reading and writing proficiency tests. In addition, formative evaluation will take place through the school year. Each team will write a plan to improve literacy; I will make periodic visits to the schools to be sure that the teams are following their plans. I will speak with the students and watch them in action to determine their effectiveness with students being tutored. Following selected visits to the university, inner-city middle school and junior high school students and the undergraduates will complete evaluation forms to determine the effectiveness of the Shadowing Day and other activities taking place at the university.

Dissemination: We will share information about the program at state and national conferences and conventions (for example, NCTE and IRA) as well as through publications of NCTE and IRA so that others who wish may adapt Teens for Literacy in their schools.

Budget: To implement Teens for Literacy as described above, we are seeking the following:

Personnel

Honorarium for 10 teachers (@$500/teacher)	$5,000.00
Honorarium for each student in the program during the school year (@ $5/month/student for 9 months for 50 students)	2,250.00

Materials

For each school to use in tutoring or in other ways to improve reading and writing (@ $500/school)	5,000.00

Transportation

For five visits from 10 schools to the university (@ .31/mile)	1,000.00
Travel for director to go to schools during school year paid by the university	(1,000.00)
Total Requested	$13,250.00

Once the Teens for Literacy team has been established, the next goal is to develop the tutoring component of the program. The next chapter contains practical ideas for your students to use in tutoring their peers or younger children in or around their school.

Chapter Four

Establishing an Effective Tutoring Program

The Teens for Literacy program does not need to subscribe to one single tutoring method. The activities that follow address the wide scope in reading abilities that you may face when forming your team. The method you choose is up to you. However, there are several general topics and ideas that we do address with each school team during the orientation session as well as through the year. Before we address the tutoring session, it is important to consider how the tutoring component of your program will be evaluated.

Evaluation

Evaluation is a difficult issue for many teachers. It should be built into a program or project from the beginning, although this did not occur when we began the Teens for Literacy program. But through observation and anecdotes we can clearly see the value of the program. We can see in each school we visit the teacher-liaisons and team members in action. By doing so, we are able to identify many issues that are pertinent to the program that we might not have been aware of. Examples include teacher-liaisons having to find after-school transportation for the members, finding places to tutor, and having access to a phone to return calls. What we also have seen is the excitement of team members as they prepared for tutoring sessions, or the smiles from the students as they shared their stories of a recent event they planned.

More formally, tutors keep tutoring logs in which they describe *when* and *where* they tutored and *whom* and *what* they tutored. Tutors know that they are responsible for their teams and they are proud to live up to their responsibilities. In addition, teachers interview their team members regularly.

Following is a brief explanation of some of the fundamentals of tutoring. We begin by sharing a portrait of what a typical tutoring session might look like.

A Typical Tutoring Session

Adrian opened the door to the classroom knowing that his first stop would be to Mrs. Merlino's desk. The meeting with Mrs. Merlino was very short, but important information was exchanged about Josh, the child whom Adrian tutored. In the midst of giving directions on a math assignment to her students and addressing another student's distress over a misplaced book, Mrs. Merlino shared with Adrian her observations about Josh's struggle with being able to identify the beginning, middle, and end of a story. She handed over a folder that contained some ideas for teaching the concept of a story's beginning, middle, and end. Adrian had a few minutes to look over what the teacher gave him before he started his tutoring session. He knew that he would be able to use the teaching ideas during his next tutoring session with Josh. Adrian gathered the supplies he brought with him and walked over to the far corner of the room. Josh was sitting at his desk, looking up with anticipation as Adrian approached.

"Hello Josh. How are you?"

"Fine. Are we going to read *Ziggy and the Black Dinosaurs* today?"

"Yes."

"Good."

"What did you do this weekend?"

"I played some ball—watched some TV. You know, the usual stuff."

"Well, let's go to the library."

Adrian and Josh walked out of the classroom and down the hall. From behind, Josh looked like Adrian's younger brother. They stayed fairly close to each other and laughed about something as they passed the gym.

Adrian chose a table in the back of the library nestled between two bookshelves. He pulled out a book that he had been reading aloud to Josh for the past few weeks. Josh pointed to the picture on the front cover and commented about the expressions on the boys' faces. Adrian began reading. Josh leaned into Adrian to see the picture on the page that was being read aloud.

When Adrian finished reading the chapter, he turned to Josh and asked, "So, what do you think will happen next in the story?" Josh paused for a moment and then shared what he believed would occur in the next chapter. Adrian followed by asking Josh to explain his reasoning for this prediction. Getting Josh to predict future events in the story had been a tutoring goal of Adrian's for the last few sessions. "Well, we'll have to find out what happens the next time we read together," Adrian announced eagerly.

Adrian put aside the chapter book and pulled a book from his backpack. It was a story that Josh had started reading in the last tutoring session.

"Josh, can you tell me what happened in the story so far?"

"Sure! The two best friends got into a big fight with each other. The one boy with freckles said that it was his friend's fault because he made fun of him. They went to talk to the teacher about their problem."

"Good! You really remembered the important details. Now I would like you to think about the problem of the story. We talked about this last week. I want to show you a way that can help you figure out what's happening in the story—it's called a story map."

"Like a map of a city?"

"Sort of—but this is a map to a book. I'll show you one that I did for a story that we've already read together."

Adrian showed Josh a completed story map that had the problem of the story labeled, as well as the sequence of major events, and the conclusion of how the problem was solved.

"Josh, we are going to try to make a map for the story you are reading now. Here is a blank story map. Write in next to the word problem what you think the conflict of the story is."

Adrian and Josh worked together for several minutes writing the conflict of the story. Adrian asked Josh to continue reading the next chapter. When he was done, they talked about what happened. Adrian asked Josh to identify the main event of that chapter. Josh did so and he wrote this on his story map. They continued discussing the book until they were interrupted by the sound of the bell, signifying the end of the period and the conclusion of the session. Both boys quickly packed their backpacks and said their good byes.

What Is Tutoring?

Tutoring is the process in which a tutor and a tutee engage in and interact with literacy experiences. The idea of a literacy experience is quite encompassing. Essentially, it is any material, activity, or event that provides an opportunity for literacy growth. This could mean reading a book, taking a trip to a library, writing about a movie seen over the weekend, or meeting a children's book author. A tutor is the person assisting the tutee in developing literacy skills and strategies by creating and implementing the literacy experiences. The tutee is the person who is learning from the tutor; however, the tutoring experience is not unidirectional. The tutor learns a great deal from the tutee, and the two participants often develop a close relationship.

There are two main types of tutoring: peer tutoring and cross-age tutoring. In peer tutoring, the tutor and the tutee are of a similar age or grade level. Usually the tutor is regarded as being more skilled in reading or writing. By pairing the two students, their age similarity helps the tutor relate to the tutee in a way that an adult might not. Cross-age tutoring involves two persons who are different in age or grade level. Usually, the tutor is the older student who knows more about reading and writing. Cross-age tutoring relationships tend to be more prevalent because of the members' interest in working with younger children.

Current Efforts to Promote Tutoring

In recent years the U.S. education system has been criticized for not being able to meet the needs of the country's children. Newspapers run headlines proclaiming real or imagined educational atrocities. Regardless of the validity of these perceptions, they have resulted in a movement that encourages and promotes tutoring as a way to enhance education.

There are many successful tutoring programs that have been initiated in the United States. Here are two examples:

America Reads Challenge. U.S. President Bill Clinton has established this program to encourage a national grass-roots effort of families, communities, schools, and libraries to improve the reading and writing skills of U.S. children. The program's goal is to help children read well and independently by the end of third grade. America Reads is structured on the idea that children learn best with a partner who can provide individualized instruction and attention; in other words, a tutor.

Rolling Readers USA. This program was founded in California by a father who began volunteering to read to people in homeless shelters after he saw how much reading aloud to his son improved his reading ability. The program has two major components: reading aloud in the community and tutoring. Volunteers read aloud to children and adults in schools and community centers. Volunteers can also tutor a student in grades 1–3 an hour a week. Rolling Readers volunteers also distribute books purchased with donated money to school children.

Why Does Tutoring Succeed?

The active learning that is involved in tutoring surpasses any passive approach to learning, including those using technological advances and strong teacher-directed lessons (Foster-Harrison, 1997). Active learning is a term that is used widely in education to describe "learning by doing." This contrasts with passive learning in which the learner's role is to absorb information presented by another individual. In active learning the learner is directly involved in the learning process through activities, discussion, and responding to what is being learned. This manifests itself in a tutoring session through read-alouds, responding emotionally to the literature, discussing the success of a comprehension strategy, or even encouraging the tutee to choose his or her own books to read. Students enjoy reading aloud with first the tutor reading a page and then the tutee reading the next page. It is the interaction between the tutor and the tutee that enhances this active learning; both are an integral part of the process.

Audrey Gartner, codirector of the Peer Research Laboratory at the City University of New York Graduate Center, has observed that

> the use of intensive student-to-student tutoring has the advantages of providing successful role models and of being less expensive than tutoring provided by teachers or other adults. It also provides a double benefit, since tutoring helps both the student being tutored and the tutor, who learns by teaching someone else. (Gartner, 1999)

How Are Tutoring Program Goals Established?

One of the first steps in creating a successful tutoring program is to determine the program's major goals. These goals should be what the collective group of the members—the tutors, the teacher-liaison, and possibly the tutees' teachers—decide are the over-arching objectives of the tutoring sessions. You do not need to develop a mission statement or anything as complex as that, but establishing goals should involve serious thought and discussion, which should take place before the start of the tutoring sessions so the tutors will have a clear idea where they are heading. Some examples of program goals follow; please note that some goals are general while others are specific depending on the needs of the tutees and the desires of the team.

- Helping the tutees to become better readers
- Helping the tutees to engage in the reading-writing connection
- Helping the tutees to decode words in the text they read
- Helping the tutees to better comprehend the texts they read
- Helping the tutees to become more fluent readers
- Helping the tutees to enjoy reading for pleasure
- Helping the tutees to read a variety of genres and topics
- Helping the tutees to see how reading is a part of everyday life
- Helping the tutees to see how reading benefits themselves and their community

Later, during the tutoring-planning sessions, ask whether the activities that occurred in the past few sessions were successful in approaching these long-term objectives. If the activities were successful, they might be shared with other tutors through discussion or an activity log. Compiling these ideas in an activity log that can be shared within the school team and with other school teams is a way to promote idea exchanges. You also should examine with tutors how activities planned for future tutoring sessions reinforce the overall tutoring program goals. This might be accomplished by creating a planning worksheet for the members to fill out before their tutoring sessions.

Choosing Tutees and Pairing Them With Tutors

You have designated the number of members who are participating in the tutoring aspect of Teens for Literacy; the next step is to identify the tutees. In most circumstances it is through the joint effort of the teacher-liaison and the team members to determine what grade level or age to draw from for tutees. Because of a connection with another teacher prior to the establishment of the Teens for Literacy tutoring program, you may preselect the class that tutees will come from. If this is not the case, then seek suggestions for tutees from the teachers of the designated grade level. Usually there are more recommendations for tutees than there are tutors. It is then left to the discretion of the school team to determine how the situation should be handled. Following are some suggestions for choosing tutees:

- Does the student need additional assistance outside of what is being given in the classroom?
- Is the student willing to participate?
- Are the student's parents or guardians willing to have him or her participate in a tutoring program?
- Does the student's schedule permit participation in a tutoring program?

After the tutees are chosen, then the pairing begins. There is no magic formula for pairing a tutor with a tutee. It is very much a decision based on personal knowledge of both the tutor and the tutee and knowledge of their schedules before, during, and after school. There are no recommendations that we can make concerning whether or not it is better for the tutoring relationship to match students who are similar in gender or ethnic background. In our Teens for Literacy program, the success of the tutoring relationship is based on the individual personalities of the tutor and the tutee. Most often it is the schedules of the two participants that determine their pairing.

It is helpful to be aware that not all teachers are supportive of having their students miss instructional time for a tutoring session. Take the responsibility of ascertaining which teachers of the tutor and the tutee are willing to dismiss them from their classroom for tutoring if they have multiple teachers throughout the school day. Compare the schedules of your tutors and the tutees to find out which times match up. Next, if you are knowledgeable about the personalities of your tutors and the tutees, try to pair those who are most similar. For example, pairing a shy, soft-spoken tutee with an extroverted and talkative tutor might not result in the best combination. Remember that there is not one single best way to match partners. If you find out a few weeks into the tutoring program that a tutoring partnership is not working, despite attempts to improve it, be flexible enough to make adjustments. Doing so benefits the tutor, the tutee, and you.

Building a Relationship Between the Tutor and the Tutee

The relationship that develops between a team member and his or her tutee is at the core of what tutoring is about. At a minimum, the two spend a half hour or more together each week engaging in literacy experiences. Traditionally, we think of the member taking on the role of a mentor and the tutee as a learner. In reality, both learn from each other because of the interactive nature of these literacy experiences. Therefore, the development of an interdependent and safe relationship is important to the tutoring process.

One of the first aspects of tutoring you should discuss with team members is developing rapport with their tutees. Role playing is an effective tool for helping students explore how to develop a tutoring relationship. We encourage the members to explore their partnership with their tutee during the orientation session in which all the school teams are involved. We divide the members into small groups of four or five students. If you do this activity with just your own school team, pair members rather than have them form small groups. Each group is responsible for resolving a scenario involving meeting their tutee for the first time.

Some scenario examples include the following:

- You have just met your tutee for the first time. He acts very shy. He does not tell you anything except the answers to the reading questions you ask him. What are some things that you can do to get to know him better?
- You and your tutee have been working on vocabulary words, but he is not interested in what you are doing. It seems that all your tutee wants to talk about is basketball. He tells you about

the game he watched last weekend, who his favorite player is, and even what team he wants to play on when he grows up. How might you get him interested in learning some new vocabulary words?

- You and your tutee have been reading a book about turtles. Every time she gets to the word *shell* she cannot seem to read the word. After her fourth try, she slams the book on the table. What do you do to try to help her get over her frustration?

The members spend about 10 minutes in their groups discussing how they might deal with the situation as a tutor. Then they share their ideas and their solution with the other groups by role-playing the situation. It should be emphasized that there is not one right answer to the problems. Because each individual tutoring relationship is different, so are the approaches to building one.

Finding something that interests the tutee helps the tutor developing a rapport with that person. Encourage the members to ask questions about the tutees' likes and dislikes. Once a member discovers something that excites or interests the tutee, he or she can use this to promote further conversation. The tutees enjoy someone asking questions about them because it makes them feel important.

We firmly believe that the recognition of a person's own life experiences is important in the learning process. It places value on the learner as a part of his or her own educational journey. Many students who are tutored have not enjoyed much opportunity outside their schools to explore what literacy is, such as going to a local public library, meeting children's book authors, or having an adult read the daily newspaper to them. We try to encourage our members to start with what the tutees already know and then build on this throughout the course of the tutoring.

As the relationship continues, there are some general guidelines that a tutor should follow to maintain its development. One of the most difficult for the tutor to understand and then implement is to encourage the tutee to work and think independently. In doing so, the tutee gains confidence in her own ability and skills so that she can begin to use them outside the tutoring session. Some behaviors that contribute to this confidence include the following:

- Be supportive of the tutee. Encourage tutors to acknowledge the tutee's successes, regardless of how small or large they are. A struggling reader might not always be aware of when she is successful at integrating a new strategy into her reading or writing process. When the tutor makes her aware, it increases the likelihood that she will use this strategy again.

- Give the tutee ample time to respond. Jumping in too early to assist a tutee can promote a dependence on the tutor for assistance. Waiting is just as important in tutoring as it is in teaching. Practice with your tutors waiting at least 5 seconds for the tutee to respond to a question before giving the tutee additional prompts.

- Encourage discussion between the tutor and the tutee. Discussions should be equally balanced. Because the tutor is often more comfortable sharing information about herself, she may tend to dominate conversations during the sessions. Enabling the tutee to communicate his own interests, feelings, or responses to texts is important in creating a safe place to practice communication skills.

- Build respect and trust. The relationship that develops from tutoring is a partnership that requires both participants to respect each other. This involves more than just getting to know each other. It also means an acknowledgment of each partner's opinions regardless of the fact that one might not agree. It also means encouraging both the tutor and the tutee to be courteous to each other by notifying the other person (and the teacher) if he or she is unable to be at a tutoring session.

These are difficult aspects of the tutoring process to teach the team members if they are not aware of them already. However, they are lifelong skills that extend beyond their experience as tutors in the Teens for Literacy program.

Evaluating the Tutee's Needs

Before instruction in a tutoring session can begin, the tutor needs to be informed about the tutee's reading needs. Often assessment is overlooked as a pre-instructional tool because of the perception that it is only a means for evaluating a student's progress *after* instruction. Being aware of a student's strengths and weaknesses can provide more information for you to build on during instructional time. With regard to tutoring, this assessment should be observationally based by the tutor rather than by administering several formal reading tests.

We have found that many of our team members are already aware of the guiding principles of reading as well as the strategies that can be used by readers. We have provided a brief listing of some of the behaviors, strategies, and responses of a reader that can be observed by a tutor. These are certainly not all of them, but they can serve as a framework for beginning observation.

Emergent readers

- Do they hold the text correctly with the front cover of the book facing them and the book spine facing their left side?
- Do they read from left to right on a page?
- Do they read from the top to the bottom of a page?
- Do they use their fingers to follow the words as they read?
- Do they use picture clues to figure out the meaning of a word?
- Do they use the context of a story to figure out the meaning of a word?
- Do they make predictions as they are reading the story?
- Are they able to follow patterned stories?
- Are they able to sequence the events in a story?
- Do they know the difference between letters, words, and sentences?

Proficient Readers

- What do they do when they get to a word they don't know?
- Can they use context to understand the meaning of a word?

- Do they recognize the beginning, middle, and end of a story?
- Can they accurately retell the story?
- Do they exhibit fluent reading when reading aloud?
- Can they identify the main idea of a text?
- Can they relate the text to their own personal experiences?

Advanced readers

- Can they make inferences from the text?
- Can they identify the author's voice?
- Can they critically analyze the content of the text?
- Are they comfortable reading different genres of text?
- Can they identify the elements of literature in the text?

Giving tutors opportunity to practice observing before their first tutoring session is highly recommended. This works well in a team meeting of the teacher-liaison and the members. You should spend time discussing with the members the rationale for the informal assessment of their tutees.

Structure and Content of a Tutoring Session

A tutoring session usually lasts about 30 minutes. There are some basic elements that most school teams decide to incorporate into a tutoring session, such as having the tutee read aloud to the tutor, spending time assisting the tutee with a strategy that he or she is having difficulty with, creating some writing, and reading aloud to the tutee. The length of the session will depend on the needs, age, and availability of the tutee. The rule of thumb is the younger the tutee, the shorter the session.

Most tutoring sessions open with the member asking the tutee to read aloud. Most of the texts that are read are books that have been introduced during classroom instruction or books the tutee enjoys.

The success of being able to read something well starts a tutoring session on a positive note. It gives the reader the confidence to venture into some unfamiliar territories later in the session during some of the direct instructional time. Hearing the tutee read also helps the team member better understand some of the reading difficulties that the person might be experiencing. Keep in mind that reading difficulties are not limited to pronouncing words correctly. Readers might also have trouble understanding what they are reading, both literally and inferentially. It is also important to recognize that some of these problems with reading might arise from the contextual environment that the person is reading in or even the attitude that the tutee has toward reading. Listening in on a tutee's read-aloud is just one way to frame that reader's reading abilities.

The skills and strategies that are addressed in the direct instructional period of the tutoring session are determined by a conglomeration of the tutee's teacher's suggestions, the recommendations of the teacher-liaison, and the team member's observations of the tutee. In some schools the tutee's teacher meets with each team member before the tutoring session and specifically tells the member what to focus on during the tutoring session. One teacher in our program developed a diagnostic checklist for the members to use when working with their tutees. In some cases you may want team members to address a general need of the students they are tutoring, such as developing a desire to read. The members also make individual decisions about what to focus on with the tutee for direct instruction. Many of these decisions are based on information gained during the introductory read-aloud session.

Following are some of the skills and strategies to focus on depending on the literacy level of the tutee:

- recognizing letters, words, and sentences
- being able to decode words using phonics
- using contextual clues to determine the meaning of a word
- using pictures in a text to derive meaning of the text
- learning the directionality of text

- sequencing a patterned story
- making predictions
- recognizing the language of books; for example, "...and they lived happily ever after."
- effectively reacting to the text (reader response)
- responding to one's own responses
- finding the main idea of a text
- identifying the structural elements of literature; that is, plot, setting, characters, mood, etc.
- summarizing a text
- critically analyzing the context of a text
- understanding the author's purpose for writing
- relating the text to personal experiences

Many teacher-liaisons emphasize the importance of using the tutoring sessions to get the tutees excited about reading. This is why the time spent reading aloud is emphasized. Many younger tutees do not have a lot of literacy experiences at home and have not had the chance to develop comfort with reading fiction or informational material. This comfort could be familiarity with the structure of a story (for example, knowing what "Once upon a time..." leads to), feeling like they are good readers who can actually decode and make sense of a text, or understanding some of the written information presented.

A Tutor's Toolbox

A tutoring toolbox is the foundation of an experience that can yield excitement and interest. A tutoring toolbox consists of the supplies that a tutor should always have plus some special materials in order to be prepared for any literacy event. A tutor cannot always foresee when the interest of a tutee spontaneously leads to the making of a book. Following are some ideas of what you might encourage your tutors to carry in their own tutoring toolboxes:

- a few texts (picture books, informational passages, poems, etc.)
- writing utensils that are age and skill appropriate
- lined paper
- unlined paper
- a few sheets of construction paper
- crayons or colored pencils
- markers

These supplies can be stored in a canvas bag, a paper grocery bag, or even a small plastic container. The canvas bag works well and can be purchased for a reasonable price.

The texts in a tutoring toolbox should be changed regularly so that the tutee gets an opportunity to read many different stories. Usually for one tutoring session there should be a story for reading aloud by the tutor, a text for the tutee to read, and some additional texts that are activity-related or may be for pleasure reading.

What Texts Are Used in Tutoring Sessions?

There are some essential items that should be included in the materials that a tutor and a tutee use during a tutoring session. Not surprisingly, texts are at the top of the list. Usually, these texts are fictional storybooks or chapter books.

One of your roles is to help develop a tutor's ability to make informed text selections. Texts for the tutees should be selected based on the tutee's interests and reading level. The simplest way to determine a tutee's reading interests is by asking. A tutor could ask a tutee questions such as:

- When you have free time for reading, what types of stories or books do you like to read?
- Who is your favorite author?
- What is your favorite book?
- Other than reading stories, what do you like to read?

- If you go to a library or a bookstore, what kinds of books do you pick out?
- What do you enjoy doing for fun?

Students will be candid about their answers, especially younger children. The responses can be used to make informed choices about what texts are chosen for a tutoring session.

Children like to read about topics in which they are interested. This does not mean that all texts selected by tutors have to be of interest to the tutee. In fact, all books should not be of interest. Tutoring sessions provide an excellent opportunity to expand a tutee's exposure to various kinds of texts that deal with diverse subject matter. Knowing a tutee's current interests can help build the foundation from which to work. For example, if a tutee really enjoys stories about horses, then a tutor might begin by selecting poetry about horses. This might expand into reading some informational passages that explain how horses are used for various purposes in different cultures. The tutor could then suggest that the tutee read a picture book about the ride of Paul Revere. This might lead to other related strands that eventually have little to do with horses but are still of interest to the tutee. By carefully selecting reading materials, the tutor can still meet the interest needs of the tutee. In so doing, the tutor enables the tutee to experience many genres of texts with a wide variety of subject matter.

Another consideration for selecting an appropriate text is checking to see if it is in the tutee's range of reading ability. For example,

- Ask the tutors to remember the books they read at their tutee's age (or at their current age if they are a peer tutor). Although they might not have been or are not at the same reading level, it might trigger memories about general reading levels of texts read at that age.
- Ask the tutors what aspects of reading might be difficult for a student at a certain age.
- Give students some recommended reading lists for students of various reading levels.

There are other texts besides books that are used to foster the literacy experience including common objects such as cereal boxes and videotapes or audiotapes of children's book authors reading aloud their own stories. Members recognize that reading is not just confined to a storybook but also the labels on the packages of foods we eat, the keys of a computer keyboard, forms that must be filled out, or signs they see in their own environment. Writing also is used in a tutoring session to help students develop a complete picture of literacy. Reading and writing are interrelated, so it is important for team members to include writing in their tutoring sessions. The tutees may make their own books, write poems, respond to pictures using descriptive words, or write lyrics to music. All this helps build the reading-writing connection that is so fundamental to literacy.

Some team members use newspapers and magazines as a tutoring tool. Using these texts is a natural way to bridge the gap between school and home (being sensitive to the fact that there might not be newspapers in some homes). Many newspapers are available for free or inexpensively. Students can examine the large display advertisements. Who is the audience? In the classified advertisements, tutors can ask what the abbreviations stand for. What is being bought and sold? Examine other sections. The sports section is extremely popular for many students. Reading newspapers involves your students in reading all areas of the curriculum.

You also can ask team members to try writing a news story with their tutee. You will have to explain the difference between a news story and a short story. In a news story, each sentence is a paragraph, and the climax comes at the beginning rather than toward the end. Show students that a news story is like an inverted triangle with the first sentence containing the most important information with each of the following sentences containing information of less and less importance. Let students know that the writer of the story is not the same person who writes the headline, because it is the editor who decides if the story will appear in one column or more on a page.

Ask your friends and students to give you their magazines to do similar activities. Ask students to examine the advertisements. Who is the audience for the advertisements in *The New Yorker* compared to the audience of the advertisements in *Sports Illustrated*?

In both newspapers and magazines, ask team members how photos are used. Examine the comics sections. Then you can make your own newspapers and magazines and share them with the children and their parents and guardians, or both.

Activities Incorporated Into Tutoring Sessions

There are a wide variety of activities used in tutoring sessions. The selection of these activities should be based on the needs of the tutee as determined in the assessment phase and through ongoing observation. What we have provided is just a sampling of some of the more common activities selected for tutoring.

Read-alouds. We encourage the tutors to read aloud texts they enjoy or find interesting in addition to what the tutee is familiar with. We have heard many stories of members searching their own homes for childhood books that had been tucked away for years. Reading such books helps introduce tutees to new genres of literature, and it increases their comfort level with print. Not surprisingly, the members share texts with the tutees that turn into vibrant stories when they are their own personal favorites. They often use character voices, an enthusiastic tone, and share with the tutees their personal feelings about the story. In so doing, they contribute to a positive and interactive literacy experience.

Discussing literature. Talking about a text can be a great way to help make the story come alive to the reader. Tutors can begin book discussions with some basic questions such as:

- What do you think the story is about?
- Is there anything in the story that you did not understand?
- What did you think about the story?
- Did you have a favorite part of the story?

Once a tutee feels comfortable answering these questions, then the tutor and tutee can engage in more interactive discussion. Some topics or elements that tutors and tutees might focus on are character development; perspective of the characters; personal reactions to the characters, setting, or mood; and criticisms of the author's writing.

Retelling the story. For tutees having difficulty comprehending a story, retelling it through conversation or writing is an effective strategy for learning how to organize the events of a story. This can easily be prompted by the tutor asking the tutee to retell the story in his own words. For more advanced methods of organizing plot events, the tutee can identify the beginning, middle, and end of a story. This can be accomplished by writing a few sentences or a short paragraph about each and then illustrating them in a book.

K-W-L comprehension strategy. This is a organizational tool for tutors to use with tutees having difficulty understanding and engaging in informational text. Prior to the introduction of the text to the tutee, the tutor prepares a sheet of paper that is divided into three columns: The first column is labeled *K*, the next *W*, and the last *L*. The *K* column stands for what the tutee already *knows* about the topic of the informational text. Once the text is introduced, the tutee brainstorms what she knows and writes these ideas under the *K* column. Next, the tutee thinks of what she *wants* to learn about the topic, and records this in the *W* column. Once these two columns are completed, the tutee reads. After reading the text, the tutee writes what she *learned* in the *L* column. This strategy encourages the tutee to be actively engaged in the informational text before reading it while assessing her knowledge of the topic.

Writing books. The tutees are engaged in creating their own stories by writing and sometimes illustrating books. Simple books can be constructed with lined or unlined paper and a sheet of construction paper. These can be folded in half to make a book with pages and a cover. There are many other ways to construct a blank book. *Making Books* by (Chapman & Robson, 1991) is a good resource for ideas.

The writing can be self-directed by a tutee, prompted by a tutor, or a combination of both. Once a book idea has been chosen, the tutor and the tutee discuss how it will be developed in the writing of the story. Then the writing begins with the tutee working one page at a time. The amount of assistance by the tutor depends on the tutee's skill and comfort level. Once the tutee has completed writing the story, she should be encouraged to re-read the book, editing it as necessary. Finally, if the tutee wishes, she can illustrate her book. Supplies such as scissors, glue, magazines, crayons, markers, and a stapler should be made available, and the book can be shared with teachers, parents, friends, and classmates.

Sentence creating and cutting. This is a writing activity used with tutees who are beginning to write words and sentences. The tutee either works independently or with the tutor to form a sentence and then write it on paper. Thicker writing material such as sentence strips work well. Once the sentence has been written, the tutee reads it several times until he is able to read it fluently and correctly. Then the tutor cuts the sentence into phrases or individual words. The tutee then puts the sentence back together. This can also be done with individual letters to form words.

Letter writing. Writing a letter is a skill that takes time and practice to develop, especially among younger children. With the advent of e-mail, tutees have even more opportunity to write letters. Letter writing can be incorporated into tutoring sessions in a meaningful manner by enabling the tutee to write letters that are relevant. A tutee can compose letters to relatives, friends, community members, and even businesses.

Response to pictures. Pictures and photos from magazines, newspapers, books, art portfolios, and calendars can serve as writing prompts. Tutors can show tutees something that is visually interesting, such as a picture of a town parade on a hot summer day. The tutor asks the tutee to respond to the picture by writing. The tutor might frame the writing task by asking the tutee to write about what he believes is happening in the picture. Or write some dialogue for the characters in the picture. The tutor can specify the purpose of the writing if necessary.

Magnetic letters. When tutors are working with emergent readers who are just beginning to make the letter-sound connection, magnetic letters can be used as an activity for reinforcing this concept.

Beginning readers can manipulate the letters to make words. They also can be used in isolation to practice phonetic relationships. What is especially unique about the letters is that working with them requires some physical interaction on the part of the tutee. For some learners, the kinesthetic involvement is just as important, if not more important, than the visual or auditory part of the activity. In addition, the tutees have the opportunity to play with language by composing words using their understanding of sounds.

Worksheets. Worksheets that are written by teachers or developed professionally by publishing companies are sometimes used in tutoring sessions to help a tutee practice a specific reading or writing skill. The worksheets come from a multitude of sources and deal with a variety of skills. In most cases, they are incorporated into the tutoring sessions at the request of the tutee's teacher. Educators may argue about using worksheets but, as mentioned earlier, many students like the structure and, if done well, the activity can reinforce skills and even help develop new ones. They also provide the tutors with a springboard for beginning their sessions.

Reaching Parents

Most of the interaction and support from parents centers around their picking up their child at school if there is an after-school meeting or field trip to a university or community partner. Some schools invite parents to informal breakfasts with the principal. Over coffee and donuts parents can share ideas that are written on large papers taped to the wall. Some examples follow.

Reaching parents
1. Write in breakfast dates on the school calendar and in the school handbook.
2. Send one early mailing with all the breakfast dates for the school year.
3. Send frequent reminders home the rest of the year.
4. Develop a phone network.

5. Remind parents frequently of the importance of Teens for Literacy.

Reaching children

1. Explain to them and show them that education is important.
2. Explain that they are responsible for their actions.
3. Explain how they are responsible for their learning.
4. Sign agreements delineating roles and responsibilities of students, teachers, and parents/guardians.

Supporting parenting

1. Help parents who want to help their children with their homework.
2. Match high school and college students with parents who want to know how to tutor.
3. Make a parent center where parents can relax with their child.
4. Help parents meet teachers to see what is going on through their eyes.

Reaching parents and principals

1. Provide a list of all the activities and support available to children.
2. Encourage good behavior.
3. Trust and respect teachers and the principal.
4. Know where the principal stands on issues.

Further information on ways to involve parents—and how to obtain corporate support—is provided in Susan Gray's article "Literacy: All in the Family" (1997).

This chapter has dealt with the conception and a step-by-step implementation of Teens for Literacy in your school. It also has focused on money—what to do with it and how to get it for your program. Once your Teens for Literacy team has been established, you may consider ways to reach out to form a partnership. This is the focus of the next chapter.

Chapter Five

Visits to a University

This chapter focuses on visits to universities; however, as we have emphasized throughout the book, many of the ideas are applicable to other community partners.

Because an objective of Teens for Literacy is to encourage students to continue their education beyond high school, teams of teens and their teacher-liaisons visit a university campus five times during the school year. This is becoming more of a challenge because we need to work around the testing days at the middle schools and junior high schools. Fortunately, we get a schedule of the common testing periods for our local schools well in advance.

You can adapt these ideas to your own school team depending on the needs of your school and community. It will be helpful if you can arrange with a nearby college or university literacy educator or community member to serve as the liaison between your school team and the institution. This person can help lead you to university resources and arrange campus visits. The way our program operates is Allen oversees all aspects of the program from his base at the university, and a graduate assistant oversees the day-to-day activities, such as arranging for university visits and ordering needed materials requested by teacher-liaisons. As often as possible we visit the teams in their school during the year. A university educator will usually be willing to serve as a liaison for your Teens for Literacy program because of the benefits of the program from the university perspective. If a university is not interested in altruism, it might be interested in promoting the fact that it has connections to local schools, that it gives back to the community, that it is involved with minorities, and that the program may provide research-related ideas for professional publication.

Following is a description of the campus visits developed to meet our needs. Our afternoon meetings usually begin at 1:00 and finish around 2:30. Again, do not hesitate to change the program to fit your own circumstances.

Orientation Session

The orientation session is the first opportunity for the school teams to visit a campus. Our session usually takes place in late September or early October. Packets that include detailed directions to the university, the agenda, and other pertinent information are mailed to the teacher-liaisons during the first or second week of September. The teacher-liaisons transport themselves and their team members to the campus in the early afternoon for the meeting. We feel it is important to include the team members in this session. This has been extremely beneficial because it impresses on the members that they are an essential part of the process.

When the students first arrive they are usually hesitant to speak or smile, but it does not take long for this to change. Before everyone arrives for the meeting, we try to talk to as many of the school teams as possible. After introducing ourselves, we usually get the shy statement, "My name is...," accompanied with a nervous grin. After some time and careful nudging, the conversation blossoms into a detailed account of the enjoyable car ride to the university.

We have discovered that all we need to do is keep asking questions of the students until we find something that interests them. The shyness quickly disappears with just a little attention. There was one young man who could barely make eye contact with anyone when he introduced himself. He was asked, "Have you ever been here before?" He immediately jumped into a happy explanation of how his brother's friend attends the university. He explained that he came to campus with his brother to visit the friend. They walked around and saw a football game. He then expressed his own interest in attending college. It is through these kinds of conversations that we have begun to realize how important a connection with a university is for many of these students. Not all receive the support at home to continue their education. Just being on a university campus helps make the idea of college more likely.

The first third of the orientation meeting is dedicated to introducing the Teens for Literacy program to the school teams from the perspective of the university. We show a video of a news report about Teens for Literacy that appeared on a local television station. It gives the visitors a general overview of the program and demonstrates the impact they can make in their schools and communities. They are amazed that Teens for Literacy has received such recognition, which sparks their enthusiasm. Some ask if they might appear on television.

These students then get a preview of what the other four visits to the campus will be like for the rest of the school year. Without fail, when Shadowing Day is explained, the excitement jumps even higher (this campus visit is described in detail later in this chapter).

It is important to make the teacher-liaisons and team members aware as soon as possible of the meeting dates for the rest of the school year. Doing so helps in the massive amount of coordinating that it takes to avoid visits during schools' standardized testing and occasional field trips. In addition, the teacher-liaisons may need time to make arrangements for other teachers to substitute in their classrooms. Sometimes scheduling can be frustrating, but the availability of university classrooms and support adds to the flexibility.

The next part of the meeting is spent dealing with tutoring. It is much more effective to actively involve team members in some discussion about tutoring rather than lecturing about what they should and should not do. The goal of this discussion is to have the students brainstorm their own tips on tutoring. By this meeting most have already participated in a few tutoring sessions and have questions and ideas as a result.

Members tend to work in a cooperative group that is their own school team. Although it is nice for members to meet other members from different schools, it is important to build a strong relationship within each team. Not every member of a school team knows one another, especially in the middle grades. Furthermore, each school team has a different approach to tutoring, which enables the team to consider their unique way collectively. Members, with the teacher-liaison acting as facilitator, come up with answers to the following questions:

- What are some ways to improve a student's interest in reading?
- What are some ways to improve a student's interest in writing?
- What are the characteristics of a good tutor?
- How can you make sure a student is understanding what he or she is reading?

After the groups have enough discussion-time, the teams share their ideas. Usually, their responses are in line with what is considered appropriate for tutoring as suggested in publications of IRA and NCTE (see, for example, Roller, 1998; Walker & Morrow, 1998).

Collectively, each group decides whether or not to include a tutoring tip on the brainstorming list that is being recorded and shown on an overhead projector. The facilitator of the discussion may try to shape the discussion by asking questions that challenge a suggestion raised. When most of the teams have had a chance to share their findings, a snapshot is taken of the overhead projector screen. This makes it easier to keep what is said. Then the suggestions are typed and mailed to the teacher-liaisons within the week.

The last third of the meeting is spent exchanging ideas about activities that are planned in each school. Most of the teacher-liaisons are not in contact with the other teacher-liaisons except during the visits to the university. This provides an opportunity to learn about activity-ideas you might not have thought of. It also enables newer groups to find out how activities that were carried out by other school teams were planned and implemented. The yearly planning forms completed by each school team for the first meeting at the university are used as reference points for discussion. At the end of the meeting, the forms are collected and kept as a progress marker.

World Wide Web Workshop

The second visit to the university, which usually occurs in mid-November, centers around learning to explore the World Wide Web (a session that can easily be led by a community partner other than a university). Computer literacy is becoming a skill that is being addressed in classrooms as schools are buying computers and software packages and are gaining access to the Internet. Team members are discovering that their tutees have an interest in the Internet. The goal of this session is to introduce the members to the World Wide Web and demonstrate how it can be used in the tutoring sessions. In addition, team members have the opportunity to view the Teens for Literacy Web site (www.muohio.edu/~bergera/teensforliteracy) if they or their school does not have access to the Internet.

The World Wide Web workshop takes place in a Macintosh-based computer lab that has about 50 workstations. The members pair with a partner and choose a station. The university is fortunate to have a computer network manager who is willing to work with large groups of students in sessions. At such a workshop there should be multiple resource persons available for answering questions and helping team members solve problems because it is extremely difficult for one person alone to try to respond to all the questions that may be raised. The bulk of this workshop is facilitated by a graduate assistant, the network manager, or a person from another department who specializes in computer instruction. If you have established a partnership with a local university, it probably will have similar resources as described. If not, local businesses, especially technology-based ones, might be willing to give a miniworkshop on the World Wide Web. At the beginning of our workshop session, the members and teacher-liaisons are briefly introduced to using Netscape Navigator, the Web browser that is available in the computer lab. Not much direct instruction is given because the purpose is to get the teams interested in what the Internet has to offer. An informational packet is compiled for this particular session. The first sheet of the packet concentrates on how to use the Netscape Navigator browser to explore the Web. This is usually the most difficult part to explain to the students because many have never seen the

World Wide Web. Much of the terminology is new and the idea behind the Web is different from books or newspapers. The minimal amount of information about browsing is given to the students so they can have the maximum amount of time exploring.

The Teens for Literacy Web site is used for demonstrating how to browse the Internet. The students love to see the pictures of past Teens for Literacy members or to find out what other schools are doing. This has become a wonderful tool to communicate among schools. After viewing the Teens for Literacy Web site, each team learns, through hands-on-discussion and step-by-step information in their packets, how to update their Web pages on the Teens for Literacy Web site. On the site each school has its own page that includes photos of team members, information on current activities and projects, and how to contact the team. Each school has the opportunity to update its page by sending information to a Web site coordinator. In your own school or district, a staff member or student who is proficient in Web production can be the person responsible for maintaining and updating the page(s).

When the students are comfortable browsing, they begin referring to the "Cool Web Pages" sheet in the packet, which is a useful resource to find interesting sites without having to do extensive searching. It is encouraging to see how the students begin with some of the sites on the list and then branch out to their own specific interests. Once the members have had an opportunity to view some of the many things the Web has to offer, the teams participate in a sharing session. This is an exciting time because most members have gone to different Web sites and are curious about where other students have visited.

From here the discussion evolves into figuring out ways that Web sites can be used for tutoring. Some members bring up the point that just by reading a book online, students become more interested in reading. One insightful team member said that even if the site is not a story that could be read online, the tutee would still be reading something he or she has an interest in. Another student built on this by saying that by having the letters in a "mixed-up" order on the keyboard, the tutee would have to be able to know the letters to type in something. A few students even found Web sites with ideas for helping others having difficulty reading and writing. By listening to the students, we discovered endless possibilities. By the end of the workshop, the members feel comfortable browsing on the Web and are familiar with ways of using it into their tutoring.

Broadcasting Facility Tour

The tour to the broadcasting facility was not always the activity planned for the third visit. In the past members have visited the university art museum or the library. After several years, though, questions about videotaping and tape recording began to surface more frequently, especially as video technology became more prevalent. The members asked if they could do audio- and videotaping and how to go about doing so. We contacted the university's communications department for help.

The decision was made to include an informational and exploratory session on recording technology. The university television and radio studio enabled the teams to learn tips on how to use the equipment and how to produce news broadcasts and programs for radio and television.

Near the middle of the school year the members begin using videotaping and tape recording as a way of checking the progress of their tutees and to view their own approach to tutoring. This is also a time when some of the literacy-based assemblies, like the book-a-thon celebration, are beginning to be planned by the Teens for Literacy teams. The teams have an interest in videotaping the assemblies for future viewing. By the time they visit campus, the members are rather excited about seeing how a real studio operates.

The tour, which is led by a professor in the university's communications department, begins with an overview of the production studio. Teams are able to see the equipment that is used during a broadcast, the steps in producing a half-hour show, and some of the roles that university students have while preparing for and filming the news. At one point everyone is squeezed into the production booth. When the cameras are turned on in the studio and the team members can see the video feed, a collective "oooh" and "ahhh" is heard. What the members also find exciting is stepping onto the news set and sitting behind the anchor's desk. Students are asked to think about the skills that a news anchor must have. Not surprisingly, they realize that news anchors must be able to read, write, and speak thoughtfully, reinforcing the notion of the importance of literacy in the working world.

We spend the last half hour visiting a nearby residence hall to show team members how college students live away from home. Then, in the lounge of the residence hall, we have a brief discussion, with pizza and soft drinks, to assess the year's progress. Members share insights about their experiences. Although the team members have visited the campus only three times, they are now ready to share some personal thoughts and feelings about their progress. This is a strong testament to the effect this program has on the members. They begin to feel part of a caring, learning community.

One of the more powerful stories shared was by an eighth-grade student. It had little to do with reading but a lot to do with his own personal development. Midway through the feedback session, he raised his hand and asked if he could share something. He slowly rose from his chair, briefly scanned the audience, and then began telling us that his parents always told him that he had an attitude problem and that he was not sure what they meant by this. He certainly never thought that he had an attitude problem. Then he began to tutor a fourth-grade student. He told us his frustration with this student who thought of himself as "great" and "cool." When he first began tutoring, his tutee refused to read and write, so they just talked. Several weeks later, they really began working together on reading. And then the eighth grader concluded, "I now know that I had an attitude problem because I could see myself in this kid. I didn't want to be like that. And like the kid, I changed too."

Shadowing Day

If you can do only one visit with your community partner, we suggest the shadowing because it is extremely exciting for the team members. We discuss our Shadowing Day in the context of a university setting, but it can easily take place at a local business. The goal is to have students interact with others to see what their goals are and appreciate the importance of higher education. Each team member is teamed with a college student and the two spend the day together. From 9:00 a.m. until 3:00 p.m. they go to classes, to lunch, and to other places around campus together.

Shadowing came from a suggestion of a master's student who helped the program as a graduate assistant. "Wouldn't it be nice," she said one day, "if the Teens for Literacy students shadowed undergraduates and graduate students all day long to see what college life is like?"

That first year a van was rented from the university. Early one morning we picked up the van and drove 35 miles to Cincinnati to meet the children from several schools gathered in one of the school yards. We then drove back to the university where a university student and team member went to classes, ate lunch, and visited parts of the campus together. That first year we had 21 of these pairs walking around campus. At the end of the first day of shadowing, the schoolchildren and the university students filled out anonymous evaluations. The ratings for both groups were sky-high, and now shadowing is an integral part of Teens for Literacy.

Preparations for Shadowing Day begin several months in advance of the late March event. Unfortunately, this time in the school year is usually reserved for state proficiency or other standardized testing. Once the date has been established, the number of members that are going to attend must be determined. On average, there are about five members from each school who come for the day. Permission slips and a letter explaining the details of Shadowing Day are sent to the teacher-liaison at each school. The request is that the permission slips be returned about a month before the day is scheduled. Attached to the permission slip is an "I'm going to Shadowing Day" form that asks members what they are interested in and what hobbies they have. This information is used to pair the members with the university students.

Most of the university students who participate in Shadowing Day are taking education courses so it is fairly easy to ask the professors who are teaching those classes if we can drop in during a class session and briefly "plug" Shadowing Day. As a teacher, you may not have the opportunity to solicit students at a university. If that is the case, we suggest that you contact someone at the university who can encourage students to participate in Shadowing Day. Perhaps you can ask a professor you might have known when you were a student. University students who are interested fill out a form immediately after class and are contacted within a week. Signs are also posted throughout the building where most education courses are offered. Using student interests and class schedules, the members and university students are matched with each other about 2 weeks before Shadowing Day. A letter is sent to the university students detailing the schedule for the day.

There are many details that must be attended to in planning Shadowing Day. The first is transportation. If you are driving only your school team, this is not a big issue. However, if there are multiple school teams that are traveling to a university, a school bus from a professional bus company in the area can be hired to transport the members, or you can make arrangements to use the buses from your own school district. In our situation, the teacher-liaisons do not accompany the members to the university for this visit. Team members are picked up around 8:00 a.m. at three centrally located schools. Their parents are made aware of these arrangements, and they have signed permission slips.

When the team members arrive on campus at about 8:45 a.m., they receive a packet of information for the day. It includes a sheet with both their name and their partner's name on it, a day-long schedule, a list of ideas of what the pair can do during the day, a reimbursement-for-lunch form, and two evaluation sheets to be completed at the end of the day. From here students meet their partners and then disperse around campus. There are many opportunities for getting to know the campus; these include eating in the dining hall and taking a tour of the sports/recreational facility.

The day concludes with a half-hour feedback session in one of the classrooms. This gives the partners a chance to say goodbye to each other, grab a quick snack that we provide, and fill out evaluation forms. Some of the partners exchange addresses and promise to keep in touch. The team members are impressed by different things. One was amazed that there are so many buildings at a university. She said that she thought a university was in one building. Many students remark how tired they are from walking around all day.

What is really exciting about this feedback time is that we get a chance to see how a student's confidence has grown over a period of 1 or 2 years. Following a college student helps to picture themselves in a university setting. The experience becomes personal. Many of the students have told us after participating in Shadowing Day that they want to go to college, and that is why we arrange for someone from the admissions office to share information on tuition aid and scholarships. (See the newspaper article on Shadowing Day shown in Figure 2.)

Recognition Luncheon

Every year the students and their teacher-liaisons go above and beyond in time, effort, and dedication to the Teens for Literacy program. To honor them we end the school year with a luncheon at the university. You also can do this with your community partner. It is a culminating experience highlighting the successes of the year and looking forward to the future. At the luncheon each team takes about 5 minutes sharing high points of its activities. If we have a speaker–for instance, one year our speaker was Sharon Draper, the U.S. teacher of the year–we ask each team to make posters illustrating their activities so others can look at them leisurely.

Not only are the teacher-liaisons and the members invited, but their principals are invited to the luncheon as well. We also invite a few friends and members of the university and local community who know the program. As a courtesy we send invitations to state school board members and state and national lawmakers. These dinners are

Figure 2

Shadow Day: Miami students show campus life to youngsters

By Ryan Weber
Journal-News
OXFORD

In the Monday sunshine, shadows trailed everyone strolling the Miami University campus.

But Kelly Link, a Miami senior from Dayton, found herself accompanied by a shadow of a different shade: Jamie Akers, a Cincinnati seventh-grader eager to learn about life on a college campus.

Link spent the entire day with Akers, taking her to class, treating her to lunch and getting to know her "shadow."

Akers had joined about 35 other "shadows" from various Cincinnati middle schools who boarded a

Greg Lynch/Journal-News

Jamie Akers, left, a seventh-grader from Schwab Middle School in Cincinnati, spent Monday shadowing Miami University senior Kelly Link.

(Continued from Page A1)

tour the campus and receive training in subjects such as exploring the World Wide Web.

This year nine schools — Garfield Junior High School in Hamilton, Verity Middle School in Middletown and seven Cincinnati schools — participated in Teens for Literacy, Shafran said.

Miami recruits Teens for Literacy volunteers from among students enrolled in

the university's School of Education and Allied Professions, Shafran said. The student volunteers work directly with the seventh-and eighth-graders, often as tutors in the middle schools.

"When they're student-teaching, they can have 35 kids facing them, and they don't get that one-on-one experience," Shafran said. "Shadowing gives the students an opportunity to find out what seventh- and eighth-graders are really like."

The middle-school students arrived in Oxford at about 9 a.m. Monday. They soon were matched with Miami students who share their interests, Shafran said.

That's when Akers met Link.

Later, at about 2:30 p.m. — nearly time to board the bus back to Cincinnati — Akers described her day with Link as "nice."

"We went to a computer class, and she taught me how to print out papers with

bus to Oxford Monday morning to participate in Miami's annual Shadowing Day.

The event, now in its third year, allows seventh- and eighth-

> 'She had no idea what college was like, but now I think she has an understanding.'
>
> Kelly Link
> Miami senior

graders to experience hands-on a day in the life of a college student, said Liz Shafran of Miami's School of Education and Allied Professions.

"It helps to get students involved with the university," Shafran said. "There are tours,

drawings," Akers said. "Then we went to her house and had lunch and went to the bookstore."

Link, who majors in special education at Miami and is the youngest child in her family, said she enjoyed spending the day with someone younger.

"It's been great getting to know each other" she said. "She had no idea what college was like, but now I think she has an understanding."

Shafran said Akers' new

opportunities to meet professors — but Shadowing Day is a great way for students to see concretely what happens in university life."

She said Shadowing Day is part of Miami's Teens for Literacy program.

Teens for Literacy, launched eight years ago by Miami professor Allen Berger, aims to encourage inner-city students to improve literacy in their schools and neighborhoods, to attend college and to consider teaching as a profession.

Students involved in Teens for Literacy visit Miami about five times each year, Shafran said. The students attend luncheons,

(Please see MIAMI, Page A2)

understanding of the college experience illustrates what Shadowing Day is all about.

"This is an important program because they are gaining valuable experience in a university setting," Shafran said.

"Having this experience prior to attending college will encourage them to continue their education. It also gives them confidence, because they become familiar with the university setting."

Used with permission from *The Cincinnati Enquirer* /Sue MacDonald.

normally for more than one school, but you can do the same on a smaller scale to honor your own school team. Restaurants are good locations for this as well as a room in a local community center. You might even want to invite all parents of the team members and tutees and their parents, as well as supporters of the program in your school.

When Henry Jung, who obtained the funding from alumni to support the original Teens for Literacy program, announced his pending retirement in 1998, we invited each school team to prepare a 5-minute thank you to Henry in any way they wished. Each team found a creative way to honor Henry at the annual recognition luncheon in April 1998. Henry accepted the teams' poetry, posters, and prose with graciousness. Later he wrote the following note to us:

> How can I ever thank you and Liz for the pleasant surprise. As I listened to the students present their statements of appreciation, I couldn't help but reflect back to the countless number of students who participated these past 9 years. We can all be proud of their contributions and the inspiration of the teachers supporting their efforts and involvement. Teens for Literacy was then and is today a wonderful program.

Throughout this chapter we have shared activities to engage in when visiting a university or other community partner during the school year. In the next chapter, ways to implement Teens for Literacy in more than one school in your district are presented.

Chapter Six

Literacy Beyond the Individual School

This chapter focuses on the Teens for Literacy program from the viewpoint of the university as a larger program coordinator. Many of the ideas also apply to anyone in a middle school or junior high school interested in spreading the program to other schools.

From the university perspective, you will have to support why the university should participate in a program like Teens for Literacy. You may have your own honorable reasons; for example, the program is helpful to children and teachers. But universities do not often make decisions based on the common good. So you will need to have ready a few other reasons of a more selfish nature, such as the program focuses on minorities, many more minorities may consider enrolling in the university, and the university will get positive press. With these thoughts in mind, here are suggestions for the realization of a region-wide program.

Selection of a School

The first step in establishing a region-wide Teens for Literacy program is the designation of the school(s) involved in the program. The selection of a participating school is of vital importance. A criterion is that the school needs additional support and resources. Currently, nearly all our Teens for Literacy schools are in inner cities.

It is helpful if a participating school's educational philosophy is congruent with the philosophy of Teens for Literacy. Reading the district's or school's mission statement is a way to gauge if the philosophy and goals are compatible. This also can be determined in a brief conversation with a district or school administrator.

Another criterion for consideration as a participating school is the physical proximity to a partner educational institution. It may be unreasonable to have a distance of more than an hour between the two locations because the driving time might take away from valuable instruction time in school.

In the first year of our program there were three schools that were involved. All three met the above criteria and were enthusiastic about piloting the program. Involving two of the schools was a relatively simple process. The principals were contacted and meetings were arranged. It was a little more difficult to begin the program in the other school, the largest of the three. After phoning the district's central office, a letter was sent and considered by the school administration. Eventually the district granted permission to call a designated school and make an appointment to meet the principal, and then we received permission to move ahead with the program.

Making Contact With a School

There are several preliminary steps to follow before the Teens for Literacy program in each school can really take flight. Once a school has indicated an interest in the program, meet with the principal or assistant principal.

The ideal time for this meeting is soon after the start of the school year. Teachers, students, and administrators will then have the opportunity of participating in the program for the full yearly cycle. Although this might seem obvious, it is important to have a face-to-face meeting with the administrator rather than conducting the meeting through e-mail or over the telephone. The support of the administration in each school is so paramount to the success of the program that it is essential to create a good rapport early.

There is a lot of talk now about partnerships between schools and colleges. But many partnerships tend to consist of the colleges dictating to the schools; in other words, in many places the situation is not equal. What we try to do is involve teachers, students, and principals in ways they can tell what works best for them in their own schools and neighborhoods.

Some issues that should be touched on during the initial meeting include the introduction of the Teens for Literacy program; an explanation of what the program entails for teachers, students, and principals; deciding how the teacher-liaison at the school will be selected; and some of the logistical details that are particular to that school. In some places the idea of students tutoring other students is such a radical concept that many questions are raised about what prompted the development of the program. It is at this point that the program objectives are explained.

Once an understanding about the principles of the program has been reached, the conversation usually shifts to specifics. Two roles that need the most definition are the teacher-liaison position and that of a team member. Teacher-liaisons are the link between a university and individual schools and thus their role is extremely important.

Designation of a Grade Level

Tutoring another person on a consistent basis requires a great degree of responsibility. Sometimes the Teens for Literacy member tutors or is involved in a literacy-promoting activity without the constant direct supervision of a teacher. For example, in one program, team members walk a few blocks to an elementary school where they tutor. They do so without their teacher. Because of the maturity of these students and their strong feelings of loyalty, they are responsible enough to supervise themselves. Many teacher-liaisons spend a great deal of time at the onset of the school year establishing ground rules. In general, this has been effective in preventing problems. In fact, many members who have been labeled as behavior problems show a dramatic behavioral change throughout the year. Many teacher-liaisons attribute this to the relationship between the team member, the tutee, and the accompanying successes.

The grade level that this program is targeted for can be modified to fit your own needs. Currently, we are exploring the impact of expanding this program to the high school level. Teens who have been in the program as middle school or junior high school students, and who are now in high school, expressed a strong interest in continuing to be part of the program.

A suggestion for a Teens for Literacy program in the elementary school is to focus more on tutoring and less on other activities. Doing so will help concentrate your team's energy on one manageable element of the program. You can achieve this by having students work with children who are in other classes within the school. For example, a fourth-grade student can help a second-grade student learn to write short stories. By doing so, teens will not only be tutoring but also improving their own literacy skills.

Selection of the Teacher-Liaison

The selection of teacher-liaisons is usually done by a school's principal who may have several teachers in mind. The teacher-liaisons tend to be language arts or reading teachers, but any interested teacher or counselor could fill the role. Some of the attributes of a liaison that work well with the program are enthusiasm, dedication, creativity, communication skills, and flexibility. We asked several of the teacher-liaisons how and why they got involved with Teens for Literacy. The most common response is that they heard about it from another teacher who had seen the program in action in a different school, or had seen the program itself by taking classes at the university. Teacher-liaisons thought the program would help meet the literacy needs of their school and community. Additionally, many of the teacher-liaisons recognized that the program might be a good way to build leadership in their students.

Once the opportunity to participate in Teens for Literacy is announced, there is usually more than one teacher interested. When there is a strong interest on the part of several teachers, or if there are scheduling complications, two teachers can share the role as co-teacher-liaison. Most teachers continue their role as a teacher-liaison for multiple years because of their strong belief in the program. There are several current teacher-liaisons involved in Teens for Literacy that have participated in the program from nearly the beginning.

Lessons Learned

Let us mention a few mistakes we have made that might help you in implementing Teens for Literacy at one school or multiple schools. These points may seem minor, but they are issues that you may experience when participating in the program for the first time.

1. Be careful of who you select as a speaker. Some may have experience teaching college students but little experience with teenagers, especially from the inner city. On one occasion we arranged for a person from the university to talk with the teens in the computer lab. The teens were sitting at computers and the speaker was standing in front of the room giving a lecture about the history of computers and how they work. The students were eager to begin working. Finally, after about 20 minutes (a third of the time) the speaker asked the teens to turn on the computers. What she was saying was important, but it could have been woven in more efficiently. Talk with each person who may be speaking with the teens in your program. You may have to explain that teens are not like typical college students.

2. Reserve a room for your end-of-year luncheon at least a year ahead of time to be sure that the room can accommodate all you plan to invite.

3. Be sure that each team can fit into the car the teacher-liaison drives. Our first year one principal became so excited he signed up nine students—four for the fall semester and five for spring. The only trouble was that the first four liked the pro-

gram so much they did not want to leave, so the second semester we had nine students. For each of the remaining meetings a van was rented from the university, driven to the school, and students were picked up and returned to the university.

4. Be sure that when you bus students for Shadowing Day that you have one or more chaperones on the bus. On one occasion a teacher noticed that there was no chaperone except the driver. She became alarmed and insisted that her students not go, and then an administrator who overheard her said none of the children could go. As a result, that visit had to be rescheduled and an enormous amount of planning had to be redone.

5. Remember to write thank-you letters to everyone involved in the program throughout the year.

6. Remember to evaluate your program on a regular basis. Ways to do so are presented in Chapter Seven.

Proof of the Program

This chapter deals with broad issues that affect the individual school teams and an overall program that consists of multiple school teams. In Chapter Four we discussed how to get parental involvement and support for the program. Here we focus on how to evaluate the success of the program and ways to get the word out to others about Teens for Literacy.

Encouraging Words

Teens for Literacy meets the needs of a wide range of students. The program allows a great deal of freedom for those who participate to design and implement activities and tutoring lessons that best fit their own situations. I chose this particular program design because I like simple ideas, and this is a very basic, powerful idea that can be put into practice easily. Does it come from research? It is possible. But my feeling is that many teachers and administrators are ahead of researchers, because it often is the practitioners who come up with ideas and then researchers (usually college students or professors) confirm the value of the ideas. Let me emphasize that there is nothing wrong with this: It is encouraging to learn that what you are doing is supported by research. We have provided a variety of suggested readings in the Appendix; you will find these articles support the use of tutoring as a means to improve literacy in schools and communities.

Sharing Stories

Students' successes are noticeable in other ways. One teacher-liaison has noticed that her team members have been attending school regularly since the start of their participation in the program. This trickles down to the tutees who are sure to be at school the days they are tutored. Another teacher-liaison meets regularly with his members to discuss their journal responses written after each tutoring session. He has seen them develop leadership skills and confidence in their ability to help others. People outside Teens for Literacy have expressed their observations. During a field trip to a local farm, one of the representatives from the farm said that he had never seen such a good relationship between younger and older students. Some of the stories are somewhat humorous. One teacher-liaison laughs every time she hears her team members talk about how their tutees "didn't even pay attention to me" during a tutoring session. Suddenly, the members get a glimpse into the lives of teachers!

When Numbers Count

But these stories are not enough for many people, particularly politicians. They want numbers. They want evidence of quantity as well as quality. Here are some of the ways to provide this kind of evidence.

- Count attendance to support the program's effectiveness. Is there an improvement for students in the program? Count the students staying in school and those taking and passing benchmark tests.

- Count those graduating. These are the kinds of numbers easily accessible and understood by politicians and the public.

- Gauge the quality of the program from the public. Teens for Literacy has been highly praised by the public through newspaper articles and television programs.

- Obtain completed questionnaires from team members, from those they have tutored, from teachers of the tutees, from the teacher-liaisons, and from the school principals. The following responses support the program's success.

> From a student team member's questionnaire: "In five years I hope to be in college pursuing my dream to major in veterary (sic) science. I do hope to have a part-time job. Teens for Literacy helped me know more about teaching and working with people."

> From a tutee: "I get better grades in all my subjects."

> From a teacher-liaison's questionnaire: "TFL has made me consider ways that I can effectively promote literacy at our school. I have gotten involved in very worthwhile activities where I might not have been involved without TFL."

> From a school principal's questionnaire: "The Teens for Literacy Program sponsored in our school by Mrs. Becky Lawson [teacher] with the support of Dr. Allen Berger has been a tremendously successful project in promoting literacy in our building and community. Students have sponsored book fairs and Right-To-Read Week Activities, tutored other students, published student writings, donated books to various classrooms as well as community agencies. In addition our students have certainly benefited personally from being in leadership roles, assisting others, and being exposed to the opportunities available on a college campus. We are very fortunate to have the Teens for Literacy program at Garfield."

• Trace students who have participated in Teens for Literacy. Most participants should respond superlatively.

• Consider the use of standardized competency tests to assess a student's ability to read and write. Although somewhat controversial, these tests provide a benchmark for a group's success. Using test scores prior to participation in the Teens for Literacy program and comparing these group scores to later scores may provide some indication of growth and success.

So Does Teens for Literacy Work?

Teachers who have kept track of students in the program report that *all* have passed the proficiency tests required to graduate from high school. One teacher reported that she has had a total of 42 team members over 6 years. She said that all 42 students had "near perfect attendance" in contrast to many other students in her school. In regard to test taking, she wrote that "their grades, test scores, attitude, and cooperation all have soared." All 42 have graduated and 14, she said, planned "to go to college to be teachers." We have also traced students who have been in Teens for Literacy during the early years; many of them have gone to college; others who chose to go into the workplace after high school have found stable jobs. They all report the value of Teens for Literacy in helping them work well with other people at work or in college.

The following is a representative questionnaire returned from a graduate of Teens for Literacy (responses are in italics).

Dear Former Teens for Literacy Participant,

We started another year of Teens for Literacy this past fall and are grateful to all of you who helped get the program started and made it successful. We would appreciate your taking a few minutes to give us an update about yourself. A return envelope is enclosed.

1. How many years did you participate in Teens for Literacy? *Two*

2. Are you still attending high school?   yes   *no*
   Did you complete high school?   *yes*   no

3. Are you currently working? If so, where? *Yes, I work at the Cincinnati Air Conditioning Company.*

4. Where else have your worked before? *Union Terminal-Tour Guide, Pharo Trucking, Red Lobster, Primavista, University of Cincinnati (in the pathology lab)*

5. Were you involved in any activities in high school? If so, which ones? *football*

6. Have you or are you currently attending any college or trade school? If so, what school and for what degree or certification? *I'm not, but I'd like to get a degree in computers.*

7. How did your involvement in Teens for Literacy affect you? *It helped me learn to work with people.*

8. Do you have any suggestions for Teens for Literacy? *I just hope that the program keeps going. It's a great experience.*

I really enjoyed Teens for Literacy. I must thank you for the opportunity to be a part of it. I didn't get your last letter because I'm out of town a lot. Right now I'm in Louisville, KY, doing a job that's been going on for 5 months.

I'm getting my diploma through home tests & schooling. I hope to get in somewhere with a good computer program. I think you are doing a great thing with Teens for Literacy. It teaches people a lot.

Spreading the Word

It is important to share good news about Teens for Literacy. You can do this inside and outside the profession.

- Write a proposal to appear with your team at a state conference.
- Write a proposal to appear with your team at a nearby national conference.
- Create a Web site.
- Talk to the education reporter of a local newspaper.
- Talk to a key person at a local television station.
- Talk to a key person at your public radio station.
- Offer to speak about your Teens for Literacy program at a luncheon meeting of a local Rotary, Kiwanis, Optimist, or Lions Club.
- If you are connected with a college or university, meet with someone from their public information office.

Over the years the program has had a great deal of positive publicity. Photographic essay albums along with videotapes of teens tutoring young children are helpful when visiting potential donors. As a result of successful proposals, teachers in the program have given presentations at annual conventions of IRA and NCTE.

When the program first began, we thought that only the teens on the teams were affected positively. But you will learn as we did that not only are the team members excited; their excitement carries over to their tutees as well as teachers, principals, and nearby colleges and universities.

Afterword

Teens for Literacy is a program that began in inner-city schools, but you can just as easily set up the program in suburban and rural schools. Teachers and principals from a variety of school settings have phoned, written, and e-mailed us for information. Some have organized teams of teens in their schools. Some teams of students graduating from middle schools and junior high schools have continued the program in their high schools. In other words, you can do it! Give it a try! And, if you have a chance, let us know how it goes. Have a great year!

Allen Berger
bergera@muohio.edu

Elizabeth Shafran
liz@shafran.com

Resources for Readers

Suggested Readings

Berger, A. (1996, February/March). Teens for literacy. *Reading Today*, pp. 36–37.

Berger, A. (1997). Writing about reading for the public. *The Reading Teacher*, *51*, 6–10.

Berger, A. (1997, April/May). Let's mend fences with our newspapers. *Reading Today*, p. 37.

Boylan, H.R. (1999). Exploring alternatives to remediation. *Journal of Developmental Education*, *22*(3), 2–10.

Cairney, T.H. (1992). *Other worlds: The endless possibilities of literature*. Portsmouth, NH: Heinemann.

Capossela, T. (1998). *Harcourt Brace guide to peer tutoring*. New York: Harcourt Brace.

De La Paz, S., & Graham, S. (1997). Effects of dictation and advanced planning instruction on the composing of students with writing and learning problems. *Journal of Educational Psychology*, *89*(2), 203–222.

Doake, D.B. (1995). *Literacy learning: A revolution in progress*. Bothell, WA: The Wright Group.

Fagan, E.R. (1967). Literature and the disadvantaged. In E.R. Fagan (Ed.), *English and the disadvantaged* (pp. 85–93). Scranton, PA: International Textbook Company.

Foster-Harrison, E. (1997). *Peer tutoring for K–12 success*. Bloomington, IN: Phi Delta Kappa Educational Foundation. (ERIC Document Reproduction Services No. 408 283)

Graham, S. (1997). Executive control in the revising of students with learning and writing difficulties. *Journal of Educational Psychology, 89*(2), 223–234.

Greaney, K.T., Tunmer, W.E., & Chapman, J.W. (1997). Effects of rime-based orthographic analogy training on the word recognition skills of children with reading disability. *Journal of Educational Psychology, 89*(4), 645–651.

Hancock, J. (Ed.). (1999). *The explicit teaching of reading.* Newark, DE: International Reading Association.

Herrmann, B.A. (Ed.). (1994). *The volunteer tutor's toolbox.* Newark, DE: International Reading Association.

Kozol, J. (1991). *Savage inequalities: Children in America's schools.* New York: Crown Publishers.

Maloney, M.E., & Buelow, J.R. (1997). *The social areas of Cincinnati: An analysis of social needs* (3rd ed.). Cincinnati, OH: Urban University Planning Program of the State of Ohio/University of Cincinnati, School of Planning.

Maxwell, M. (1990). Does tutoring help? A look at the literature. *Review of Research in Developmental Education, 7*(4), 1–5.

McCarthy, J. (1999, March 31). Volunteer-tutoring bill receives governor's signature. *[Hamilton] Journal-News,* p. A12.

Morrow, L.M., & Young, J. (1997). A family literacy program connecting school and home: Effects on attitude, motivation, and literacy achievement. *Journal of Educational Psychology, 89*(4), 736–742.

Pinnell, G.S., & Fountas, I.C. (1997). *How America reads.* Portsmouth, NH: Heinemann.

Pumfrey, P. (1991). *Improving children's reading in the junior school: Challenges and responses.* London: Cassell Educational Limited.

*READ*WRITE*NOW! Activities for reading and writing fun.* (1995). Washington, DC: U.S. Department of Education.

READ*WRITE*NOW Partners Group. (1997). *Checkpoints for progress in reading and writing for families and communities.* Washington, DC: U.S. Department of Education.

Rose, M. (1989). *Lives on the boundary: The struggles and achievements of America's underprepared.* New York: Free Press.

Schmahl, C.M., & Thorkildsen, T.A. (1997). Conception of fair learning practices among low-income African American and Latin American children: Acknowledging diversity. *Journal of Educational Psychology, 89*(4), 719–727.

Sheldon, W.D. (1969). Problems of reading instruction in an urban society. In D.L. Cleland (Ed.), *Reading in an urban society* (Report of the 25th annual conference and course on reading, pp. 7–14). Pittsburgh, PA: University of Pittsburgh.

Showers, B., Joyce, B., Scanlon, M., & Schnaubelt, C. (1998). A second chance to learn to read. *Educational Leadership, 55*(6), 27–30.

Stanovich, K.E. et al. (1997). Converging evidence for phonological and surface subtypes of reading disability. *Journal of Educational Psychology, 89*(1), 114–127.

Thomas, A., Fazio, L., & Stiefelmeyer, B.L. (1999). *Familes at school: A guide for educators.* Newark, DE: International Reading Association.

Topping, K. (1987). Peer tutored paired reading: Outcome data from ten projects. *Journal of Educational Psychology, 7*(2), 133–145.

Wentzel, K.R. (1997). Student motivation in middle school: The role of perceived pedagogical caring. *Journal of Educational Psychology, 89*(3), 411–419.

Suggested Viewing

Shooting for Success. Based on the film *Stand & Deliver* about the achievements of Jaime Escalante and his students in inner-city Los Angeles. Available from the National Education Association, 1201 16th Street NW, Washington, DC 20036. (22 minutes)

Socrates for Six-Year-Olds. Matthew Lipman encourages young children and abused teens to tackle tough philosophical problems. Emotional tension mounts in the classroom, but children of all ages, backgrounds, and intellectual aptitude demonstrate how both their attitude toward learning and their achievements in the classroom benefit from philosophical inquiry. Available from Films for the Humanities & Sciences, Box 2053, Princeton, NJ 08543-2053. (60 minutes)

Literacy Organizations

International Reading Association (800-336-READ). With more than 90,000 members in 99 countries, IRA has a wealth of helpful information in publications (including electronic) and conventions that support teachers of literacy. (Web site: www.reading.org; Address: 800 Barksdale Road, PO Box 8139, Newark, DE 19714-8139)

National Council of Teachers of English (800-369-6283). With more than 70,000 members in the United States and countries around the world, NCTE provides a wealth of helpful information in publications and conventions that support teachers of language arts and literacy. (Web site: www.ncte.org; Address: 1111 W. Kenyon Road, Urbana, IL 61801-1096)

National Reading Conference. This is an organization of approximately 1,000 reading educators who are among the most prominent researchers in the literacy field. NRC publishes the *Journal of Literacy Research* and a yearbook of annual conference presentations, and copublishes a book series, titled the Literacy Studies Series, with IRA. (Address: PO Box 809130, Chicago, IL 60680-9130)

There are other important organizations in literacy that do not have a permanent address. One such organization that has been around for many years is the National Conference on Research in Language and Literacy (formerly the National Conference on Research in English). People have to be invited by a member to become a member, and they meet informally at the annual conventions of NCTE and IRA. The organization produces occasional publications relating to research in literacy education available through NCTE.

Other Resources

Accelerated Reader Program
Advantage Learning Systems, Inc.
PO Box 8036
Wisconsin Rapids, WI 54495-8036
800-338-4204
www.advlearn.com

Junior Great Books
Great Books Foundation
35 E. Wacker Drive
Suite 2300
Chicago, IL 60601
800-222-5870
www.greatbooks.com

Pages Book Fair
801 94th Avenue North
St. Petersburg, FL 33702
800-729-2080

Scholastic Book Fair
www.scholastic.com

Troll Book Fairs
100 Corporate Drive
Mahwah, NJ 07430
800-446-3194
www.troll.com/bookfair/index.html

References

Berger, A. (1997, April 9). Snapshot of an inner-city school. *Education Week*, pp. 44–45.

Chapman, G., & Robson, P. (1991). *Making books*. Brookfield, CT: The Millbrook Press.

Draper, S.M. (1994). *Ziggy and the black dinosaurs*. Ill. J. Ransome. Orange, NJ: Just Us Books.

Gartner, A. (1999, September 9). Letter to the editor. *The New York Times*, p. A24.

Gray, S. (1997, February 6). Literacy: All in the family. *The Chronicle of Philanthropy*, pp. 9–10.

Roller, C.M. (1998). *So...what's a tutor to do?* Newark, DE: International Reading Association.

Walker, B.J., & Morrow, L.M. (Eds.) (1998). *Tips for the Reading Team: Strategies for Tutors*. Newark, DE: International Reading Association.